BY LARRY MCMURTRY

Literary Life: A Second Memoir
Rhino Ranch
Books: A Memoir
When the Light Goes
Telegraph Days
Oh What a Slaughter
The Colonel and Little Missie
Loop Group
Folly and Glory
By Sorrow's River
The Wandering Hill
Sin Killer
Sacagawea's Nickname: Essays on the American West
Paradise
Boone's Lick
Roads
Still Wild: Short Fiction of the American West, 1950 to the Present
Walter Benjamin at the Dairy Queen
Duane's Depressed
Crazy Horse
Comanche Moon
Dead Man's Walk
The Late Child
Streets of Laredo
The Evening Star
Buffalo Girls
Some Can Whistle
Anything for Billy
Film Flam: Essays on Hollywood
Texasville
Lonesome Dove
The Desert Rose
Cadillac Jack
Somebody's Darling
Terms of Endearment
All My Friends Are Going to Be Strangers
Moving On
The Last Picture Show
In a Narrow Grave: Essays on Texas
Leaving Cheyenne
Horseman, Pass By

BY LARRY MCMURTRY AND DIANA OSSANA

Pretty Boy Floyd
Zeke and Ned

HOLLYWOOD:

A THIRD MEMOIR

Larry McMurtry

SIMON & SCHUSTER

New York · London · Toronto · Sydney

Simon & Schuster
1230 Avenue of the Americas
New York, NY 10020

Copyright © 2010 by Larry McMurtry

First Simon & Schuster hardcover edition August 2010

SIMON & SCHUSTER and colophon are registered trademarks
of Simon & Schuster, Inc.

For information about special discounts for bulk purchases,
please contact Simon & Schuster Special Sales at
1-866-506-1949 or business@simonandschuster.com.

The Simon & Schuster Speakers Bureau can bring authors
to your live event. For more information or to book an event,
contact the Simon & Schuster Speakers Bureau at
1-866-248-3049 or visit our website at www.simonspeakers.com.

Designed by Jill Putorti

Manufactured in the United States of America

10   9   8   7   6   5   4   3   2   1

Library of Congress Cataloging-in-Publication Data
McMurtry, Larry.
   Hollywood : a third memoir / Larry McMurtry.—1st Simon & Schuster
hardcover ed.
        p.   cm.
   1. Motion pictures—United States. 2. Motion picture plays, American—
History and criticism. 3. Motion picture authorship. 4. McMurtry, Larry.
5. Screenwriters—United States—Biography. I. Title
PN1993.5.U6M3255 2010
808.2'3092—dc22
[B]   2010018222
ISBN 978-1-4391-5995-8

Jacket photographs (top left to bottom right): © Paramount/The Kobal Collection;
© Columbia Pictures/Photofest; © Artisan Entertainment/Photofest; © Columbia Pictures/
Photofest; © CBS/Photofest; courtesy of Everett Collection; © Motown/Pangaea/Qintex/
The Kobal Collection; © CBS/courtesy of Everett Collection; © Paramount/The Kobal
Collection; © Columbia Pictures/Photofest; © CBS/Photofest; © Zade Rosenthal/Paramount/
The Kobal Collection; © Tony Esparza/CBS; © Paramount/Photofest; © Columbia Pictures/
Photofest; © Focus Films/Everett Collection

This book is dedicated to the working women
of the American film industry:
Those who hold the scripts
Those who dress the sets
Those who soothe the egos and calm the storms
With the author's love and respect.

HOLLYWOOD:
A THIRD MEMOIR

I

———————

HOLLYWOOD—AS OPPOSED TO movies, its principal product—entered my life almost simultaneously with my son, James McMurtry, who arrived in March 1962, at which time I was teaching world literature—all of it, from the *Ramayana* to Dylan Thomas—at Texas Christian University in Fort Worth, Texas. To the farm and oil patch kids I was teaching, literature—or at least my mandated selection of it—held little appeal. In desperation I began to challenge these reluctant students to Ping-Pong matches, a game at which I was then quite good. If a student won, he or she got an A; if they lost they got a C.

That may seem a little unorthodox, but then five classes is a lot of classes. Between matches I was able to make friends with two writers, John Graves and Dave Hickey, both still alive and both still friends.

Then one day a man from Paramount Studios called, taking me by surprise. He turned out to be a location scout—that night he took me to dinner at what was probably the best restaurant in Fort Worth. Though, by this time, I had lived in both Houston and San Francisco, I knew nothing of fine dining. The man wore a pin-striped suit which bespoke a standard of eloquence far beyond my own. Though the suit was probably just normal Brooks Brothers, I remember it to this day; and I also remember the news he brought me, which was that Paramount had just bought the film rights to my slight first novel, *Horseman, Pass By*, and planned to film it in the Panhandle of Texas, starting almost immediately, with Paul Newman to star. The sum they planned to pay me, $10,000, meant, to me, farewell forever to the *Ramayana* and to table tennis as a grading system as well.

The nice man wondered if I had any relatives in the Panhandle, folks who might help them with the locations. In fact the Panhandle was then chock-full of McMurtrys, and I sent the gentleman to the most able of the bunch, my cousin Alfred McMurtry, then living in Clarendon. Paramount promptly rented not only a lot of Alfred's land, but also his cattle herd and a good number of his cowboys.

Thanks to all these rentals Alfred McMurtry made a lot of money out of what became a movie called *Hud,* but I didn't begrudge him his good fortune, since he did have to put up for a while with the considerable aggravation of a movie production, whereas I did not. I was safe in Fort Worth, with a living and lively child.

I also had to finish my semester at TCU, which I had wrongly supposed would be my farewell to teaching school: in a little more than a year I was a lecturer at Rice, where I taught for almost nine years.

The moviemaking in the Panhandle began about the time I finished with TCU. Eventually I was asked to visit the set; the invitation, when it came, was issued without enthusiasm. It was as if the director, Martin Ritt, and the screenwriters, Harriet Frank and Irving Ravetch, had jointly decided to do the right thing, which, in their world, meant inviting the author to the set, though in fact the author of the film they were filming was more or less the last person they wanted to see, novelists being, after all, famously difficult about movies made from their work. They were apt to detect bruises on their text where none were intended by the filmmakers.

In my case Martin Ritt and the Ravetches need not have worried. I was there only for an afternoon, and spoke only a few words, and would hardly have been inclined to protest even if I had known what was going on, which of course I didn't. These were the people who had freed me from the *Ramayana*, which counted for much more than any blemishes in the film.

I spent most of that afternoon parked in a line of cars on a Panhandle dirt road, waiting for a man with a walkie-talkie to let us approach the set. I saw Paul Newman at a distance, but didn't actually meet him until thirty years later.

Patricia Neal, whom I really *did* want to meet, wasn't working that week; her too I met thirty years later, in the check-in line at the Beverly Wilshire Hotel. We later had a pleasant visit.

Unhappily I arrived on the day when the buzzards misbehaved: I have told this story fully in a book called *In a Narrow Grave* and don't wish to repeat it here, though the fact of buzzard misbehavior probably cost Paramount about $60,000, which put everyone in a really bad mood and dashed whatever hopes there might have been for social plans with me.

Several members of the crew seemed stunned by the fact that they weren't getting anywhere with the buzzard scene. Martin Ritt, a nice man, was so depressed by the day's output that he made no effort at all to make contact with me. Years later I met *him* in Austin.

At the end of the day the famous cinematographer James Wong Howe took a few beauty shots of my cousin Alfred's beautiful (to grass lovers) wavy grass, and the whole lot of us trickled back to Amarillo.

I was not invited to watch the dailies (raw footage, usually) but I didn't then know that dailies existed and did not feel insulted. In the next fifty years I watched more than my share of dailies. In weak moments I like to think I discovered Jennifer Garner, but that was from an audition tape, not a daily.

The Ravetches and I only spoke a few words; they were nice words but even then I heard the first faint whispers of something I was to suspect many times: the desire on the part of filmmakers that the author whose book they were filming did not exist. Ideally there should be no book and no author: if not, then the film would be *all theirs,* something that can never be the case if there *is* a book and an author.

Most filmmakers instinctively believe that authors are *always* proprietary about their books, and many are: many, but not all. I wasn't, for example, possessive, either on *Hud* or the other films made from my books. Mainly one hopes that a film of one's books will be good, but, hey, there's the money. *The author gets money!* On *Hud,* Martin Ritt was so burdened with budgetary concerns that he didn't care whether I was there or not, or whether it was my book or not, and that is the condition of most directors on most films.

They have their day to make—shooting the scenes they were supposed to get, and the kindest thing an author can do is stay out of the way and not slow them down.

I did have one authentic thrill while visiting the set of *Hud*. The little Panhandle town of Claude, Texas, was substituting for my own mythical small town, Thalia. I've used Thalia as a setting for several books, including all of the *Last Picture Show* quintet.

Driving through Claude the next morning, on my way back to my wife and young child, I noticed that the water tower in Claude didn't say Claude anymore: it said Thalia. That my invention had caused a small town in North Texas to change the name on its water tower—even temporarily—was thrill enough to me: and Hollywood provided it!

2

HUD WAS RELEASED in the spring of 1963, and did very well, not only financially but in the awards season: Patricia Neal, Melvyn Douglas, and James Wong Howe all won Oscars. There was a special showing in Fort Worth, which I attended, unlike all the stars, who were as far away from Texas as they could get.

The ending, weak in the book, was just as weak in the film. This tough old rancher Homer Bannon (Melvyn Douglas), who has weathered many tragedies and survived them, basically falls off his horse and dies. That was my fault—I yielded to my then editor, John Leggett, who felt there needed to be more suspense in the story. The screenwriters had a fine chance to correct this obvious mistake, but they declined the challenge.

The box office on *Hud* was sufficiently robust to raise thoughts of a sequel to this profitable cow. I had by this time finished my second novel, *Leaving Cheyenne,* which was set pretty much in the same locale. My reluctance did not deter Paramount, which optioned the book and hurried back to Cousin Alfred to help them film *Gid,* as the sequel was to be called. Gid was a rancher in the book, which was a kind of prairie *Jules et Jim.*

Since there was a barn-burning scene and they were in grass-fire country, Alfred closely monitored the precautions he wanted to be sure were in place.

Gid was never made under that title, or by Paramount; in time Alfred McMurtry became so apprehensive about the flammable barn that he burned it down himself, and, I believe, collected a bit of damage money.

Nothing more was heard of a movie called *Gid,* but, years later, Sidney Lumet made a terrible film from the same book, *Leaving Cheyenne,* called *Lovin' Molly,* in which, to my father's shock, the cowboys were dressed in bib overalls, which are farmer clothes. I hated *Lovin' Molly* so much that I wrote against it in *New York* magazine, supposedly a suicidal thing to do in Hollywood.

The threat of professional death was perhaps best enunciated by the producer Julia Phillips in her book, *You'll Never Eat Lunch in This Town Again,* a threat that's not even emblematically true. I did the unthinkable and yet have eaten hundreds of lunches in that town again, and anyone with much hustle and talent can always do the same. Punishing such talent as there is would soon become counterproductive; there's never enough talent to go around.

I had nothing to do with the filming of *Hud.* I just wrote the book it was adapted from. Similarly I had nothing to do with the filming of the fine CBS miniseries of my book *Lonesome Dove.* The same holds for *Terms of Endearment.* I just wrote the book! In *Lonesome Dove*'s case probably more than one hundred million people saw the film and associate me with it; but the muscle that created that film was not my muscle: it was Bill Wittliff (the principal producer, as well as screenwriter) whose muscle, along with that of the actors, producers, and crew, that made this such a beloved miniseries.

Still, to acknowledge the other point of view, I *did* write the books that made the films possible. I liken my effort to turning the key in the ignition, after which I step back and allow—indeed encourage—others to drive the car. Without me, no movie; but without all the others—including that location scout who bought me my first Hollywood-financed meal—no movie either.

The fact that *Hud* was made from my book had one extremely important effect: somehow through the illogic of show business it enabled me to get work on scripts for no better reason than that I was from the West—cowboy country.

From 1963 to the present moment I've been offered screen work, even though, at the beginning, as this narrative will demonstrate, I knew nothing about what I was doing in a craftsmanlike manner.

I learned by doing, there being no one willing to instruct me, and I will always be grateful to Hollywood for . . . well . . . it's essentially financed my fiction, my rare book business, and, to a huge degree, my adult life.

3

ONE THING I'VE always liked about Hollywood is its zip, or speed. The whole industry depends to some extent on talent spotting. The hundreds of agents, studio executives, and producers who roam the streets of the city of Los Angeles let very little in the way of talent slip by. A screening or two of a new film happens every day, and if the talent spotters are doing their job correctly, talent gets spotted before the talented person is even aware that anyone is looking.

In the Hollywood mind I believe I have always been thought of as a writer who could produce marketable Westerns—and this determination was made before *Hud* had even been released. Someone saw an early screening and liked what they saw—a few days later my phone rang in Houston—I was then back at Rice—and a voice asked politely whether I would be available to come to Hollywood and talk with a producer named Alan J. Pakula about a film he wanted to make about the Natchez Trace.

At the time I had never heard of Alan J. Pakula, but, to be fair, except for the late Mike Todd, I had never really heard of *any* producer. At this juncture, 1963, I had only been in Los Angeles once and that was a hasty trip I made to hit the legendary bookshops, of which I only got to a few, though I did make it down to Long Beach to the famous block-long Acres of Books, now ending its days, alas.

The book Alan Pakula then wanted to make was Paul I. Wellman's *Spawn of Evil*, a study of pre–Civil War outlawry along the Natchez Trace.

Apart from having crossed it a time or two in its modern incarnation, I knew nothing of the Natchez Trace. After chatting for a few minutes with Mr. Pakula's assistant, I learned that I would not be expected to adapt the whole book, itself just a number of slight studies of various outlaws who had preyed on travelers along the route for some years. What Alan Pakula wanted was a script about John Murrell, a very bad outlaw whose claim to fame was that he attempted to instigate a slave rebellion across the entire South. Paging through the book, which reached me the next day—almost everything from Hollywood usually reaches you by the next day—I discovered that the chapter on John Murrell was only eleven pages long—the same number of pages, ironically, as the famous Annie Proulx story "Brokeback Mountain," which my writing partner Diana Ossana and I were able to adapt successfully for the screen.

Fortunately the little sketch about the villainous John Murrell was filled with action, ending with the evil plotter getting his head cut off and stuck on a pike.

From my point of view the only problem was that I had never written, or even read, a screenplay. The Ravetches had not offered to show me the script of *Hud,* a copy of which I finally bought many years later from Larry Edmunds's famous movie bookshop, the general stock of which I later also bought for a bookshop I was running in Houston, earning me, I fear, the eternal enmity of Git Luboviski, wife of Milt Luboviski, with whom she owned the store.

Another thing that always works smoothly in Hollywood is travel arrangements. From Houston I flew first-class to LAX, the first of more than one hundred visits to that famous portal. I found that I liked traveling first-class so much that I continued to fly it even when I was flying on my nickel. Later I learned that Igor Stravinsky had the same habit, as did his friend Sergey Diaghilev.

Many years later, while briefly a producer myself, I discovered that travel by private jet trumps first-class by a considerable margin. Private plane travel will likely always be the luxury I enjoy most.

In the early 60s there was not the traffic on the L.A. freeways that one encounters today. On the first visit I was easily able to find my way to the hotel, the Roosevelt, on Hollywood Boulevard; I was staying there only because Mr. Pakula's assistant assured me that the Roosevelt was where writers stayed.

Later I learned that at least one writer I had heard of, William Faulkner, had stayed there, but that was probably when the Hotel Roosevelt was in its youth, which was a long way behind it when I first stayed. Since then it has sunk and risen several times, never sinking to the level of the famous Hotel Hell, only a few blocks away; on my first visit it had a tarnished quality that was hard to miss, but, on the other hand, it was only a few blocks away from the several open-till-midnight bookshops on Hollywood Boulevard. One had to dodge a good many hookers of both sexes to get to the bookshops, but I had lived in both San Francisco and Houston, neither of them hooker-free; I was a fairly adept dodger.

I must mention that I liked Hollywood from the moment I first visited it, and I like it still, even though it must be said that the traffic now is a serious problem, holding one in gridlock for long stretches, preventing one from getting where one might want to go.

As Jack Kerouac aptly said, Los Angeles is still the West Coast's one and only golden town. Say it's glitter all you want: at least it's real glitter, applied at a level that for me never fades.

4
───

When I first visited Alan Pakula he was chiefly a producer; his then current project, *Inside Daisy Clover,* was adapted from a novel of the same name by the English screenwriter and novelist Gavin Lambert. The director was Robert Mulligan, whom I confused, for a time, with the Texan director Robert Benton, who also worked with Alan Pakula.

Inside Daisy Clover was being filmed for Warner Bros., on one of their huge soundstages in Burbank. I was in sight of the action for only a few moments—just long enough to glimpse Natalie Wood, sitting in her chair and looking very very bored. Then I was whisked away to the Warners offices, most of which I would visit several times over the course of the next fifty years.

Alan Pakula was a nice man, but when I arrived he seemed preoccupied. Since he had a costly film in production, preoccupied is exactly how he should have looked, I felt, although I was not as familiar with the burdens of production as I am now.

It was clearly not easy for him to escape his knowledge that there sat Natalie Wood, bored in her chair. The Natchez Trace, as it was prior to the Civil War, and John Murrell's devilish scheme to set the South aflame, must have seemed especially distant to Mr. Pakula just then. His response to this dilemma was to send me home to write a Treatment about the Murrell plot.

A treatment, in movieland terms, is a kind of summary of the story that might be filmed, someday, if all goes well. In length they are usually twenty to twenty-five pages, although they can be a bit longer if the subject warrants it.

I didn't know this, and no one offered me the slightest advice or instruction. I was not even offered a glossary of film terms. Alan Pakula had his film to make and I had a plane to catch. It was the only time in my long experience of filmmaking that I was not at least taken, usually by the producer, to Chasen's, the famous eatery in Beverly Hills—it is now defunct. The dinner at Chasen's was for a long time an accepted part of diplomatic procedure in Hollywood.

Many years later, in another time, Alan Pakula made up for this lapse by buying me a very expensive breakfast in New York.

Thus uninstructed I went back to Houston and wrote a treatment about the Murrell rebellion that was more than four hundred pages long. I have heard that E. L. Doctorow's first script for his famous book *Ragtime* was even longer, but, quite possibly, that may not be true.

I'm sure that Alan Pakula and his team were more than a little startled when they received my bulky effort, though they didn't actually say as much. What they actually depended on was a fluke of casting: meaning that Marlon Brando had briefly come available—maybe. And maybe was about as close as a producer could get to Mr. Brando at that time.

In response to my epic treatment I was asked to alter the Murrell story so that there were actually *two* brothers, one good, one bad. Who was to play the good brother I never was told, although scuttlebutt had it as Steve McQueen, though that didn't, to me, seem very likely.

I went back to Houston and produced a shorter, though still lengthy, second treatment; it contained Conradian overtones (that was Alan Pakula's description). My second draft was a mere three hundred pages, after which *Spawn of Evil* was never heard from again, at least not by me. Marlon Brando's availability vanished as mysteriously as it had appeared.

My breakfast in New York with Alan Pakula in the early 70s was a discussion about my persistently unfilmable fifth novel, *All My Friends Are Going to Be Strangers,* an attractive story no one can figure out how to make—and it's getting on toward forty years now since filmmakers began to try.

All I really gained, in my first efforts as a writer for hire, was how to get from Warner Bros. to LAX very quickly. I was paid, I believe, $3,000 for that job—it seemed like good money to me.

5

MANY, MANY WRITERS have worked unhappily in Hollywood and come away feeling that the whole moviemaking system, both studios and independents, was somehow braced against them.

My own feeling, after working there for more than half a century, is that more or less the opposite has occurred with me. I began with no qualifications at all to be a scriptwriter, and yet Alan Pakula and Warner Bros. immediately hired me to make a start with *Spawn of Evil*, although, at that point, I had never even *seen* a screenplay. I had been to one movie set and that so briefly that I had not even had the time to sort out the terminology. What did a best boy do? A grip? A second AD?

I was a stranger in a strange land, but I was, at least, willing to learn: the problem was that no one was inclined to teach me. I was handed eleven pages and invited to do my best.

The problem of instruction was soon to change. Within a year film schools began to blossom in universities across the land; and manuals on screenwriting began to show up in bookshops. I glanced at several of these but didn't delve deeply into any of them, mainly because, despite my evident ignorance, I kept on getting jobs. Let a sheepherder in Montana peck out his memoirs and his memoir often came to me, the main reason for this being that I could evidently create characters that major actors might well want to play. That particular ability is still scarce in Hollywood. No matter that I was usually only the first stage of the rocket. I wrote the liftoff, got the actors interested, and then, usually, another screenwriter took my pages and built them into a narrative structure.

Very few of these early efforts got made. The exception was *Hud,* which went into production almost instantly, and did so for one reason only: a major star had committed to it while it was still in galley form.

This instant production has never happened to me again, despite more than fifty years of trying. I thought another piece of luck had come when Tom Hanks, through his company Playtone, optioned my little post–Civil War Western *Boone's Lick,* which contained a role that could have done for him what *Hud* had done for Paul Newman.

For nearly five years Tom Hanks seemed enthusiastic; and then he dropped his option. Stars will often do that. John Wayne could have been Captain Call in *Lonesome Dove,* though what he turned down was a very different story from the *Lonesome Dove* that was eventually made. Stars of Wayne's or Hanks's magnitude are always juggling a dozen or more options: it's almost a miracle when the one you have on offer actually gets made. This applies to female stars too.

Anyway, in the 60s, I became a busy screenwriter, if a screenwriter of a very low order. The names of the movies I wrote first scripts for have long since fallen off the tape of my memory. Unless there's something singular about the producers or actors involved, I quickly forget what I may have just written.

One I do remember was an effort to milk a little more from *Hud* by putting it on TV. I was to do a pilot, and I did a pilot. The reason I remember this effort is because the producer, a large man, drove around in a chocolate brown Rolls-Royce; he also ate a lot at the Brown Derby, which went the way of Chasen's even before Chasen's faded and died.

This man's partner was a nice young producer named Mike Wise, whom I saw now and then for years, our usual meeting place being the coffee shop of the Sportsmen's Lodge, on the valley side of Coldwater Canyon. The food was good and the waitresses prototypic of the waitresses in good coffee shops everywhere: tough and quick.

In the sanctity of the Sportsmen's Lodge, where a lot of stock contractors used to come to eat, the actor Ben Johnson among them, Mike and I hatched many promising projects, among them a Western to star Eddie Murphy; we actually pitched this notion to Jeffrey Katzenberg, then doing his thing at Disney—he dismissed the notion in the time it takes to blink, but, hey, we glimpsed Michael Ovitz as we were going out the door, the only time I ever laid eyes on that luminary, though I have often stood in supplication in the forbidding lobby of the old CAA building, on the corner of Wilshire and Little Santa Monica.

Sometime in the late 80s I lost track of Mike Wise, but I enjoyed our breakfasts and hope he's alive and well. He is one of many people I would now find it difficult to locate; in a way it's the inconstancy of almost every position or relationship that makes Hollywood the interesting place it is.

There is, for instance, Fred Roos, initially of Zoetrope, Francis Coppola's production company, whom I hadn't heard from in so long that it would be reasonable to assume that he might be dead; but no, he's very much alive and still chasing my elusive novel *All My Friends . . .* I hope Fred catches it, this time; or, if not Fred, then Polly Platt, who has been nursing a script of that story for a long time.

Peter Guber, in his glorious (or at least vainglorious) Sony years, once had shown some interest in the same book. During the Oscar push for *Brokeback Mountain* my partner, Diana Ossana, and I were on the famous Sunday-morning TV show hosted by Peter Guber and Peter Bart (the long-time editor of *Variety*). What I realized when we did the show is that Peter Guber is one of those people who age only up to a point. They just seem to stop aging, a feat most of us are unable to manage.

When Peter Bart was a producer, I once did a script for him of a fine Max Catto book called *Charlie Gallagher, My Love!*—I only did one draft, which wasn't very good, prompting Peter to give me a mild scolding. There was a cattle baron figure in the story that could have been played by John Wayne, but wasn't, for the good and simple reason that Wayne died about this time. I like Peter Bart and liked the story, though there was an edge of craziness in Hollywood then that put me off a bit. Our script meetings, what few we had, were at Max Palevsky's house and there was a *Rolling Stone*–esque tone in the place that I simply could not connect with.

Charlie Gallagher, My Love! is a sweet story about a little Italian family circus that gets stranded in the great West in the time of the cattle drives. The cattle baron buys it and sends it across the vast plains to his ranch. The troupe sets off, guided by young Charlie Gallagher, a cowboy, but they never get there. The West more or less eats the circus. The picture, if made, would be a kind of reverse *Daisy Miller*, in which old Europe is destroyed by young America.

Many years later, after Diana had become my writing partner, we got a second pass at *Charlie Gallagher*. The project was then owned by Robert Halmi Sr., with whom we had made several miniseries. We gave it our best, sent in our draft, and never heard of it again. I mentioned it cautiously when we were on Peter Bart's show, but he did not pick up the ball, which has yet to bounce our way again, though who's to say it won't, someday.

6

AFTER I HAD done four or five screenplays I began to feel that scriptwriting would become and remain part of my life forever, along with fiction writing and rare book selling. In the beginning I didn't expect to write much nonfiction, but there I was wrong. I have written a dozen nonfiction books.

I should mention that I've never scorned screenwriting—it's a necessary and honorable craft, while remaining very different from the more celebrated and studied craft of fiction.

How different? Well, for one thing, movies are sort of *talked* into marketability, if they have any, the talk being mainly between writer and producer, or writer and director, or both. Actors will occasionally offer an opinion, but these opinions are rarely heeded, until a brilliant actor-producer such as Warren Beatty wants to chime in.

But Warren Beatty is the exception, not the rule. The line producers who are responsible for the daily money flow rarely get into the aesthetics of the project either.

I began to work with Peter Bogdanovich and Polly Platt on the script of *The Last Picture Show* by insisting that, in my terms, screenwriting wasn't really *writing* at all. Writing a profile of John Ford, say, is not the same as writing the script for *The Searchers*. Peter, who was and is a fairly prolific journalist who has written a fair number of profiles, in and around making films, should know that; perhaps he does, by now.

A pulper named Frank Nugent wrote the script of *The Searchers;* I don't know how much talk there was between Nugent and Ford, but they either didn't know or didn't care that when the Quakers ran the Indian Agency in what is now Oklahoma they kept a scrupulous registry of captives, one that would have enabled the two searchers to find the little girl they were searching for in about five or six months. There were a limited number of Comanche and Kiowa bands, and the Quakers, who traded with them, would soon have known which band had Debbie.

In any case the number of suggestions made by screenwriters that directors actively adopt is probably not much higher now than it was in the era of Ford and Hawks and Hitchcock. Clint Eastwood famously took Paul Haggis's script of *Million Dollar Baby* and shot it right straight through in, I believe, thirty-seven days. Paul Haggis, if he was there, probably kept his mouth shut.

I would still argue that my distinction between writing and screenwriting holds. Of course both use words, but the words in fiction come out of silence and the words in a movie script come out of talk.

For another thing, there's the money. Fiction is an extremely cheap art when you compare it with movie production. All fiction requires is a pencil, some paper, and a good imagination. Novels can be written on a few months' rent money and some groceries. But getting money, and usually a lot of it, is the first essential in moviemaking. No dough, no show. And, if it's a Western we're talking about, $50 or $60 million might now be required; some, but not much of this, will be used to pay for a workable script.

I myself have been lucky by virtue of the fact that I have done much of my scriptwriting in decades when writers were not held accountable for the failure of a picture. And, fairly so: usually the writers weren't responsible for the failures of the cheapies they worked on—or in some cases the expensive flops they worked on either. Their salaries were minuscule in relation to what stars cost, or for that matter, what location work costs. The expense of using livestock, horses mostly, has risen so disastrously in the last twenty years as to have—for a while—virtually killed off a once popular and very profitable genre: the Western.

Over the decades I have probably written at least ten scripts that didn't get made—or haven't yet. But my partner and I are still working.

The brute fact is that most screenplays, even those scripted by well-regarded screenwriters, don't get made. As budgets rise higher and higher, it has become more and more common for screenwriters to bear some of the blame for box office failures now. In the old days, hacks (wise or unwise) would not expect to be held responsible for the various flops they worked on.

7

EVEN ON MY first visit to Alan Pakula at Warner Bros. I was aware that I was being treated a little different from the other few writers I met, and this, I believe, is because, unlike most of the young writers in the barn, I had written a *novel*. All novelists or fiction writers who went out West to do a little scripting had this edge, although they may not have realized it in time to act on it.

A published novel, whether good or bad, is at least an end product. A work of the human imagination has been embarked upon and completed. Good or bad it belongs to the writer, and has been exposed to the world as his work.

No screenplay, though, is an end product. If it's a good screenplay it may result in a produced movie. Budgets can be determined or derived from screen work and many are. Casting can begin, at least in the producers' heads, once there's a screenplay. Directors can be approached or engaged and financing can be set up. Screenplays are a vital element in the whole process but it's obvious to everyone that they themselves are not an end product. They're a blueprint that might become a building, or an orchestral score that might become lovely music.

Many writers hate this secondary nature in the film hierarchy; their complaints stretch back well over a century and continue today, but I feel no desire to add to them, possibly because I have a secure base elsewhere. There's all those novels I've written—about thirty now. If a picture I work on doesn't get made or is unsuccessful and loses money, I am not much affected. I have my other life, or lives: novel writing and bookselling.

That doesn't mean I don't work hard at screenwriting. If anything I work harder at screenwriting than I do at fiction—fiction comes to me easily, and scripts don't. I have to work at them; they're a craft I've only partly mastered—the character part. I now know what a dissolve is, and I'm more realistic about budgets than I used to be, despite which, had I not managed to persuade Diana Ossana to be my screenwriting partner, I doubt I'd be doing much screen work. She has provided the sense of structure I simply don't have. Add her sense of structure to my ability to spew out characters and you have what feels like an effective screenwriting team, not that we're the only such team under the heavens. Movies *are* collaborative efforts, a truism that's probably been uttered thousands of times. Woody Allen is the only director I know who writes his scripts alone, and even he doesn't do it all the time.

Screenwriting presents one with a constant flow of options: should the main character be a boy or a girl. Collaboration usually works because two brains can come up with more options than one brain. I knew this early on, but I didn't find Diana early on. I've worked on film scripts, most of them not bad, with Peter Bogdanovich and Polly Platt, with Diane Keaton, Cybill Shepherd, Goldie Hawn, and the fine novelist and poet Leslie Marmon Silko. These various efforts only yielded two movies: *The Last Picture Show* and *Memphis,* a film I wrote with Cybill, which was adapted by us from Shelby Foote's *September, September.* Leslie Silko and I wrote two scripts together, the unmade *Honkytonk Sue* for Goldie Hawn, and the equally unmade *Dance Me Outside,* an adaptation done for Norman Jewison from a W. P. Kinsella story; made by others, not Norman Jewison.

Diane Keaton and I labored long on an adaptation of my own *Somebody's Darling;* nothing cinematic came of this except a great friendship. *Somebody's Darling* is a Hollywood novel—it went nowhere because of Hollywood's persistent dislike of itself as a subject.

None of the above are projects that I would have taken a shot at alone. But then Peter Bogdanovich and his then wife Polly Platt came along, and the long five-book, two-movie saga of *The Last Picture Show* began.

8

THE LAST PICTURE SHOW was written in response to a family crisis, of a sort that could happen to almost any family, in almost any small town. The fact that small-towners everywhere could see themselves or their neighbors in it probably accounts for its immediate popularity.

I wrote it very hastily, in about a month, and published it in 1965.

The success of *Hud* still resonated in the marketplace and there was interest in *Picture Show,* but it was, to be fair, a pretty grim story, and the interest did not immediately rise to the level of a movie deal; and when interest did arrive it appeared in an unlikely source: a New York lawyer, whom I had met through an acquaintance in the music business. Stephen Friedman, the lawyer-turned-producer, is now dead, and I don't want to speak ill of of him, but as a producer he was, to say the least, pesky. I met Steve by accident on Third Avenue; I was in the company of a very attractive young woman and, to be polite, introduced her to Steve, who soon hit on her, as he was to do with every woman I introduced him to. In time I stopped introducing him to anyone.

Finally, with no opposition from the big players in Hollywood, Steve Friedman optioned *The Last Picture Show* for $7,500. The check bounced, but was somehow hastily made right. For the next couple of years I heard nothing more from anyone about *The Last Picture Show*.

Then, eventually, I got a script in the mail, from a writer whose name I didn't recognize and have now forgotten. It was a terrible script that somehow contrived to give this grim story a happy ending. (Later, Peter Bogdanovich and I struggled with the producer Bert Schneider over which of three deeply *unhappy* endings the film should actually end with.)

Though still pretty much a newcomer to Hollywood I knew that the script I received in the mail would never be produced. I had moved to northern Virginia by then, with my son, James, and was running a rare book business in Georgetown with my partner, Marcia Carter, who ran the Georgetown shop for thirty-two years.

I got the occasional call from Hollywood, though, and, from time to time, wrote a script. I knew that in Hollywood the order of battle was constantly changing with new heroes arriving now and then, and old heroes ceasing to be heroes and finally slipping under.

At the end of the 60s a small film called *Easy Rider* got made by a small company run by the aforementioned Bert Schneider, whose family happened to be a power at Columbia. *Easy Rider* cost not much and made a lot, besides which it also made Jack Nicholson a movie star, which he has been ever since. It was one of those highly watchable cheap movies without stars that convince the studios that it is at last possible to do away with the star system, a method of financing films that started at least as early as Chaplin, Pickford, and Fairbanks, a system that operates virtually unaltered to this day. Frankly, the most reliable way to get people to go to movies is to put people in the movie that people already know they want to see: Charlie Chaplin might be the perfect example.

I liked *Easy Rider* but I didn't expect it to be the dawn of a new day, where filmmaking was concerned. Nonetheless, the folks at BBS Productions (which included Nicholson himself for a while) rightly concluded that they could make at least one more picture along *Easy Rider* lines, and that picture turned out to be *The Last Picture Show*.

Had *Spawn of Evil* happened I might have done a lot more script work than I did, and might not have been free to do *Picture Show*. But *Spawn* didn't spawn and one of the more interesting things I did instead was an adaptation of John Barth's excellent first novel, *The Floating Opera*, which didn't spawn either, though I still like the book and wish I had been experienced enough to get the picture made.

Until *The Last Picture Show* showed up I was a try-anything screenwriter of mushroom growth. What I mainly got out of those lost projects was a little cash and many free trips to the bookshops of L.A.

9

THE MOVIE PROJECTS that came and went in the late 60s did not much affect my life, one way or the other. But late in 1970—or maybe early 1971—I got a call from Peter Bogdanovich himself, inviting me to Hollywood to talk about filming *The Last Picture Show*.

It was about that time that I suddenly became seriously interested in movies and began to fill in the vast gaps in my cinematic knowledge. I began to watch Renoir, Truffaut, Bergman, Fellini—but particularly Renoir. Since I was then in D.C. there were plenty of opportunities to see earlier films. The American Film Institute had come into being in 1967, and when the institute started a magazine called *American Film*, I was asked by my friend George Stevens Jr. to write a column for it, which I did monthly for the next two years, the results of which can be found in a book of my film writings called *Film Flam* (a title, I later discovered, that had been used by Elliot Paul).

During the year or two when I was trying to catch up on classic cinema, I did not much attend the work of the younger generation of American filmmakers, among whom, along with Coppola, Scorsese, Hal Ashby, and the like, were Peter Bogdanovich and his wife and co-producer, Polly Platt.

Peter seemed to have been a cineaste practically from the moment of his birth. He worked for the Museum of Modern Art's film department,

I believe, and then wrote a number of profiles of famous directors, most of these for *Esquire,* then enjoying the excellent editing done by Harold Hayes and his staff. Both Peter and Polly realized that the way to get ahead in Hollywood was to move there. Entry was extremely hard to gain from a distance.

So they moved there, working at first for the famous talent spotter Roger Corman (who is still spotting). Polly dressed sets, and, when necessary, made costumes. But their climb from Cormanland to Olympus is their story to tell, and neither one is at all reluctant to tell it, so I'll leave that to them. Before *Picture Show* they had made two films of significance: a documentary called *Directed by John Ford,* made for the American Film Institute, and a striking debut film called *Targets.* They shot *Targets* in sixteen days; it starred Boris Karloff, who was loaned to them by Roger Corman, I believe.

How they got from Hollywood to the dusty streets of Archer City, Texas, my hometown, is a complicated story which began when their friend Sal Mineo, murdered in 1976, gave them a paperback of the novel, the film rights then still owned by the aforementioned Steve Friedman. After the success of *Easy Rider,* Bert Schneider muscled Friedman out of the way and contacted the semi-hot director of *Targets,* Peter Bogdanovich.

Soon after that I flew out to Los Angeles where I met Peter, Polly, and their young daughter, Antonia, living quietly on Saticoy Street, not so far from where I myself came, long afterward, to live, on the lip of the Valley.

Peter and Polly kept body and soul together by cranking out a lot of film scholarship. In the early 70s many publishers began to want to publish various series relating to film: editions of great screenplays, or short biographies of famous directors. Peter and Polly did a few of these, ending, as I remember, with a book on the career of the director Allan Dwan.

On the first night of my visit Peter and Polly fed me Valley Mexican food. On the second night Bert Schneider did his duty and took us all to Chasen's, where, many decades later, I was to have my final meal with my beloved agent Irving Paul "Swifty" Lazar, who was gouty that final night and had to wear tennis shoes, a great humiliation for a man of his tastes.

On the second day of my visit with the Hollywooders I dutifully trooped over to Columbia and had the first of innumerable script conferences with Peter, through all of which he obsessively chewed toothpicks. My main memory from that day was of catching a glimpse of Marlon Brando, who had more sheer star power than all the actors in that studio put together. Though, since then, I've seen a lot of stars, Marlon Brando has still not been bested when it came to lighting up a room.

While Peter chewed his way through a lot of toothpicks we talked about various aspects of my book that either did or didn't seem to work for the film, if there was one. If we decided anything I can't remember what it was—which merely meant that we had had a normal script conference.

None of these conferences, and I have been in many, had much actual effect on the script that got written—if one did.

Back in D.C. the great Loudermilk's bookshop was being auctioned, beginning the next day. More bookman than filmmaker I flew the red-eye and attended every session with my partner, Marcia Carter.

I had gotten along fine with Peter, Polly, and Antonia, but BBS and Columbia Studios held the aces, and they were yet to show their hand.

10

Not long after my first visit to Saticoy Street, the green light went on where *Picture Show* was concerned. Many green lights, of course, end up turning red without much movement on the part of anyone. But this light stayed green, and soon Peter and Polly would be coming to Texas to look for locations. I was asked to be their guide and I accepted.

I met them at the Dallas–Fort Worth Airport and whisked them off to my hometown, about one hundred miles away. I believe I fed them in Ponder, a small town where I've been eating steak for more than fifty years. The Ranchman's Cafe, in Ponder, was no stranger to movie folk even then, since *Bonnie and Clyde* was made only a few miles away. Warren Beatty's presence was much in evidence, as was Faye Dunaway's—over the years the Ranchman's gallery of stars has grown to include Robert Redford, Lauren Hutton, Diane Keaton, Cybill Shepherd, and Cindy Crawford.

From Ponder we proceeded to Archer City itself. When Peter and Polly stepped out into the emptiness in front of the (burned-out) Royal Theatre they were so stunned that I had to push them out of the street to keep them from getting run over by oncoming traffic, just as happens to the Sam Bottoms character in the film. They had both read the book, of course, but could hardly believe, both being lifelong urbanites, that any place could be so bleak and empty as my hometown was and still is.

Indeed, the first shot of the movie happens right where Peter and Polly stood when I first brought them to the town—a move that had fateful consequences both for them and others.

The scouting trip might as well have ended right there, and I think at some level we all three realized it. After all, it's where I set the book. Wichita Falls, where the rich kid scenes were shot, was only twenty miles away, and Olney, which still had an intact movie theater, was eighteen miles in the other direction. Every location that would actually be used in the movie was within thirty miles of where we then stood, with the incessant prairie wind whirling dust around us.

Instead of saying Voilà! and calling Bert Schneider to get the trucks rolling, we proceeded to drive pointlessly around Texas for several days, looking at other towns that were a lot like Archer City.

All we did in Archer City was have dinner with my parents, who were disturbed that I had a beard—something I acquired in northern Virginia while snowed in for several days. A little later Selwa (Lucky) Roosevelt, who was later to advise President George H. W. Bush on social protocol—she was married to a Roosevelt—told me that my beard made me look like a Harvard professor, so I promptly shaved it off, though actually I have nothing against Harvard professors.

Peter Bogdanovich, who has Serbian roots, kept his distance from my parents, and, indeed, from the town, when he went back and filmed there; but Polly Platt, a WASP from Milton, Massachusetts, whose first wedding took place in Dean Acheson's house in Georgetown, soon made friends with my father and quickly became a favorite of his—or enough of one to receive lectures on the hardships of pioneer life, which his parents, particularly his mother, had experienced firsthand. It was a story my father never tired of telling.

After that memorable dinner with my parents, we three location seekers set off on a now fruitless trip, ranging as far as Matamoros, Mexico, where, in the novel, the protagonists, Sonny and Duane, go, as so many Texas boys did, to get laid.

I believe I had, by this time, produced a kind of dribble of a first draft script, an effort which Polly and I debated with some vigor, while Peter lapsed into Serbian gloom, a state he often attains. We took to the air in Corpus Christi, after a mad dash across what was, essentially, the King Ranch, and, reaching Austin, had a nice dinner with Bill and Sally Wittliff. They were at that time the publishers of my book of essays *In a Narrow Grave*. We little suspected that Bill Wittliff would soon begin an impressive film career of his own. He became, in due course, the principal force behind the miniseries made from my popular novel *Lonesome Dove*.

Then Polly and Peter went back to Hollywood and their child, and I back to northern Virginia, to my own.

I I

THAT STRANGE SCOUTING trip occurred early in 1971. During that year the script was many times rewritten. On one visit to L.A., I was idling around in Bert Schneider's office and noticed that on his desk was a small bowl of variously flavored douces. Later I saw Bert in D.C., at one of the many anti–Vietnam War protests; and, later still, I encountered him in Vevey, Switzerland, where he had traveled with Candice Bergen, and had hoped to beguile the aged Charlie Chaplin into making a film of some kind with him.

I scarcely knew Bert Schneider but I was present at the violent debate between Bert and Peter over the ending of *The Last Picture Show*. Bert didn't like the final scene, in which Cloris Leachman, the neglected wife of the local football coach, has a violent fit and then forgives Sonny (Timothy Bottoms) his near-infidelity with Jacy Farrow (Cybill Shepherd). Bert wanted the movie to end two scenes earlier, when Billy (Sam Bottoms), the local retarded boy, gets killed by a cattle truck while sweeping the street in a sandstorm.

Failing that, Bert wanted to end the film one scene earlier, when Sonny, in his grief, drives wildly off into the emptiness.

Peter won the argument and the movie ends with Cloris and her forgiveness. But the film is not quite over: following the Cloris–Tim Bottoms scene is a long reprise, in which all the characters in the story are pictured briefly at their sunniest and most winning moment.

Without that reprise *The Last Picture Show* would have been almost unwatchably depressing. I first saw it in a rough cut, without the reprise, and found it too sad to sit through.

Much later, as a stooge for the U.S. Information Agency, I toured the Southern Cone of South America with that film: thirty-two showings in Argentina, Uruguay, Chile, and Colombia (this last not of course in the Southern Cone). I didn't watch the film thirty-two times, or any times, but I did answer questions about it after every showing and I always made a point of mentioning the reprise.

The other thing that made the film so appealing was the casting: the best casting that Peter Bogdanovich, with or without Polly Platt's assistance, ever achieved. He was not an obsessive moviegoer for nothing. He was the perfect young director to be allowed to direct (and cast) a movie whose producers knew in advance that they couldn't afford stars. He had a sure sense of which actors and actresses could rise to this bait, and which couldn't.

Ironically, but not surprisingly, when Ben Johnson and Cloris Leachman won Oscars for their performances, they decided that, by God, they *were* stars, and acted like stars from then on.

The first thing they did, as stars in their own heads, was price themselves out of the market, which, Oscar or not, assessed them rather more modestly than they assessed themselves.

12

FOR A FEW months in 1971 the fate of *The Last Picture Show* hung in the balance. Little script changes were suggested from time to time, and, usually, I made them. I was more interested in our new bookshop than anything else. I had never particularly liked *Picture Show* as a novel and did not get too keyed up about its ups and downs in the studio world.

So when Peter called and told me that *Picture Show* had in fact been given a green light, I was happier for him and Polly than for myself.

By the time production started I had taken a lectureship at George Mason University, in Fairfax, Virginia, where I taught creative writing—to my surprise a good many of the story manuscripts that I received in that class were not at all vaguely S & M.

Because of my teaching duties, and the pleasures of the book business, I was on the set of *The Last Picture Show* only slightly longer than when I visited *Hud*. There was the usual morass of cameras, cables, and idle people, all chilled by the usual lacerating midwinter wind.

What I saw was a small crew working desperately to make a short deadline: in this case, Christmas. I had only a few words with Polly and Peter and was yet to meet Cybill. I made two short visits and encountered Cybill only on the second, by which time Peter had left Polly for her.

At this point in Hollywood history, long films were doing badly at the box office. For that reason the producers of *Picture Show* had decided that *Picture Show* should come in at exactly two hours, not a frame more.

To ensure that this demand was in force, the footage was timed by various arcane methods of film timing. Normally a page of script is considered to produce a minute of screen time but nobody who has actually worked in film believes that to be the case. Some writers and actors just somehow play *slow,* and my own scenes—I can't say why—play particularly slow.

By the time *Picture Show* had been in production a week it was—to the horror of everyone—timing out to be a *three*-hour movie, not the two-hour one that had been mandated.

This was calamity; back in Virginia my phone began to ring and ring. In essence what we needed to do was cut a full third of the script and do it while the movie was in daily production.

And this we did!

Not only did we do it, but it turned out not to be as hard a task as one might expect.

First we eliminated all scenes that involved bringing cast and crew to distant places.

We had at once to eliminate such temptations as San Francisco, Colorado Springs, or Matamoros, to all of which we had once hoped to go. In moviemaking the oldest truism is that money translates directly into time. So many dollars means so many days.

In *Brokeback Mountain,* for example, if Ang Lee, the director, could have had even $15,000 or $20,000 more we could have sent a second unit crew down into Wyoming for one day and got some beauty shots of the locale where the story was actually set.

He *wasn't* allowed the extra money, and neither was Peter Bogdanovich allowed any extra money as the filming of *Picture Show* neared its end. Money trumped talent, and, in the movie business, that is usually the case.

Anyway, Peter and I stayed on the phone for about a week and cut *Picture Show* by about a third, while filming went on apace. Some of the substitute scenes were better than what had been there to begin with, such as the brilliant impotence-graduation-seduction sequence. Others were, at least, no worse than the original. The film wrapped on time, and came in, initially, at about two hours and two minutes. To make that length, Peter had to cut a scene he much loved, in the café, between Eileen Brennan and Tim Bottoms. Doggedly, over the next twenty years, Peter chipped away at studio resistance until the café scene was finally put back into the release print. Since by then the picture was widely reckoned to be a classic, for once the powers-that-be relented.

13

IN DECEMBER OF 1971, I paid my second and last visit to the set of *The Last Picture Show*. When I was stopped at the one traffic light—for most of my life the only traffic light in the county—Polly Platt came running into the street to inform me that Peter had left her for Cybill—then she turned away and went back to one or another of her several jobs on the picture.

I debated where to park, rarely a problem in Archer City unless a film is in production there. In *Picture This,* the excellent documentary George Hickenlooper made about the making of *Picture Show* and its woebegotten sequel, *Texasville,* a furious young cowboy reaches his flash point when some gofer from the film crew tries to tell him where he might or might not park during moviemaking time.

Anyway, I parked, and pondered this not particularly surprising information. Peter and Polly seemed pretty married to me, and they had two children now, a second daughter, Alexandra, having been born just before the film went into production. Alexandra, along with her sister, Antonia, had been placed for the time being with Peter's parents, in Scottsdale.

I was not unaware, however, that moviemaking is hard on marriages. Pack a bunch of volatile people off to a bleak location for a month or two and romances blossom that wouldn't if the various lovers were in the safety of the suburbs.

Later in the day I finally met Cybill. In fact we sat in the car on the bridge over the Red River near Burkburnett, Texas, while the setting for Jacy Farrow was being readied, Cybill, of course, being Jacy.

As I recall, we held hands, a sign, I later learned, that Cybill was feeling shaky, as well she might have been. She was young and in a bleak place, making her first film. It was a cold day and she may or may not have just broken up (or contributed to the breakup) of the director's marriage. She would have held hands with a mule, but, no mule being available, she held hands with me.

Then the shot got set up to Peter's satisfaction and I did not see Cybill Shepherd again until she was in Miami, Florida, being directed by Elaine May in *The Heartbreak Kid.* Or maybe I caught a brief glimpse of her in Hollywood, in the Sunset Tower apartments, where she and Peter lived for a time, once it became clear that his breakup with Polly was going to take.

The crew of *The Last Picture Show* was housed in a miserable motel in north Wichita Falls. The night I arrived there was a party—it may have been the wrap party. Neither Peter, nor Polly, nor Cybill was there. I don't know where they were, but wherever it was, I think it's safe to assume that they were as miserable as the rest of us.

The Last Picture Show soon went on to glory. Jack Kroll, then the powerful movie critic for *Newsweek,* said it might be the best American movie since *Citizen Kane.* Peter Bogdanovich was made, and stayed made for a long time. He did his best to make Cybill a star, but she eventually performed that chore for herself in the sitcom *Moonlighting,* which also elevated her co-star, Bruce Willis.

14

I HAVE, IN my seventy-three years of life, rubbed elbows with a great many celebrities, both in politics and in the arts. I have seen many players become hot and then stop being hot. To those who, overnight, become white-hot, as Peter did, any cooling is unwelcome. Indeed, so powerful is the rush of being white-hot that those who are enjoying that status lose all sense that they might someday be cool. Or, worse, cold; or, worse still, frozen.

Peter Bogdanovich, while white-hot, made two other films that were also quite successful at the box office: *What's Up, Doc?* and *Paper Moon,* placing him at or near the top in the roster of young directors.

The success of *The Last Picture Show* changed a few lives forever: Peter's, Polly's, Cybill's, and the childhoods of Antonia and Alexandra.

It did not, though, change my life in many particulars. I went on writing, teaching a little, and selling rare books in Georgetown, D.C. To say that I was not missed by the Hollywood community would be an understatement. Few screenwriters have ever been *missed*: perhaps only the great Ben Hecht.

As for Peter Bogdanovich, he was happy enough for me to remove myself from the narrative of the making of *Picture Show*: most directors would be. In the making of any hugely successful film there is actually a lot of credit to divide, but I rarely see or hear of many directors dividing it. A few might say a grateful word or two if they're receiving an Oscar.

The Last Picture Show duly got nominated for a number of Oscars, including best adapted screenplay, but though Ben Johnson and Cloris Leachman won, it was pretty much the year of *The French Connection*. Ernest Tidyman, the veteran screenwriter (a position I now occupy) won rather than Peter and I. *The French Connection* also won best picture. William Friedkin, who went on to marry the great French actress Jeanne Moreau, won for best director.

In a brief cutaway to Peter, as one of the various directing nominees, he sat in his tux looking like a Serbian martyr—the only survivor of the Field of Blackbirds, perhaps.

The screenwriting nominees that year were announced by Tennessee Williams, who, when he came to me, mispronounced my name: the commonly used "McMurty." But he was a great playwright, near the end of his days, and I slipped the accidental punch.

15

IN THE FIRST of these memoirs, *Books*, I mentioned that the success of *Picture Show* made me reasonably hot on the Georgetown dinner circuit. While my heat lasted I gave my first-ever interview to a big-time journalist, in this case the youthful TV critic Tom Shales, who soon enough became, in my opinion, our best-ever critic of that popular art, television. He asked me if I missed anything about Texas, and, in order to throw him off—I missed many things about Texas—I mentioned my longing for the pink-sugar hard candy called the Peanut Pattie. In this case I underestimated the power of the press, because I was soon deluged with at least a hundred Peanut Patties, all sent from Texas by well-meaning fans.

Out in Hollywood, Polly Platt was, for a time, almost as employable as Peter, although, being a strong-minded woman who knew a lot about film production, she managed to have blistering quarrels with a number of A-list directors: Mike Nichols, Robert Altman, and Orson Welles being the ones I remember hearing about.

From time to time, if Polly and the kids and I happened to be in the same city, I baby-sat Antonia and Alexandra while their mother was at work.

Cybill, for her part, soon figured out that if she was to advance her career, she had to work for directors other than Peter. Thus her appearance in Elaine May's *Heartbreak Kid* and Martin Scorsese's *Taxi Driver*.

Peter, by this time, had purchased a mansion in Bel Air—the mansion, a sprawling white villa, had once been the home of Clark Gable's wife; and it was later to be owned by my friend Diane Keaton, who fixed it up and sold it for a lot of bucks: just the kind of thing Diane enjoys doing.

The last time I was in it, before the bank took it from Peter, it had become a kind of Grey Gardens of the West. I believe John Ford's daughter was working there then, and also Iris Chester, Peter's assistant, who had once worked for Hitchcock; meanwhile a strange crowd of Peter's old East Coast cronies: John Ritter (now gone), Ben Gazzara, John Cassavetes, drifted in and out.

Cybill was long gone by then, having retreated to Memphis and had her first daughter, Clementine.

It's my impression that Peter Bogdanovich had spent most of his youth being a puritan; with the loss of Cybill, not to mention his family, he now did his best to become a libertine. From my own observation this never quite worked.

His movies by this time (*Nickelodeon, At Long Last Love, Saint Jack,* etc.) were neither profitable nor good. From such a rise as Peter had enjoyed, some slide was inevitable—almost all successful directors fall into sloughs of cinematic failure. Only by dying young can these slack periods be avoided. Peter Bogdanovich didn't die young and hasn't died yet, but his string of huge successes had ended, and, so far, it has not revived.

There again he is not alone.

16

WITH THE POWER he gained from the success of *Picture Show* and *What's Up, Doc?*, Peter had the ability—rare and usually short-lived—to make pretty much anything he wanted to make. At first he chose films that would elevate Cybill to stardom: *Daisy Miller* (from the well-known—one can almost say "signature"—Henry James story, *Daisy Miller*). The English novelist and screenwriter Frederic Raphael was hired to do the script.

I was in and out of Hollywood then, sometimes getting jobs and sometimes not. Peter brought up the fact that there was an eleven-year-old boy in the story, Randolph, Daisy's brother. My own son, James, was eleven at the time; he was immediately, indeed whimsically, cast as Randolph. James acquitted himself well in the role: well enough that Martin Scorsese wanted him for *Alice Doesn't Live Here Anymore;* but James declined. He liked acting well enough and Europe well enough too, but the ten-day wait he had to put up with in Switzerland, where the fog on Lake Geneva stubbornly would not lift even long enough for the one shot needed.

While they were doing the Roman sequences of the story I had little to do and wandered to my heart's content through the Eternal City, which I came to love and still love.

I was working on *Terms of Endearment* then. I wrote in the mornings and wandered in the afternoon.

When the production moved to Vevey, Switzerland, I stayed in the hotel where the little story may have been conceived and walked less and read more; I also bought a small tourist rental library and shipped it home. I saw little of Peter and nothing at all of Cybill.

To assuage my son's long boredom I bought him fishing equipment and turned him loose on the quays of Lake Geneva, out of which he pulled up many minute perch. What he enjoyed more, I think, was watching the finicky old Swiss fishermen arguing over their catches.

For my entertainment I could walk the short distance down to the French border and stare at the vast Montreux Palace, where Vladimir Nabokov and his devoted wife, Vera, were living at the time. It looked to be a comfortable place, comfortable enough that the Nabokovs stayed inside. I never glimpsed either one.

In Rome we had dined once, ceremonially, more or less, with Bernardo Bertolucci, at a chilly, snooty, high-end restaurant called El Toula. Nothing was said by either young director—at least nothing I could understand.

Later that evening, though, I did glimpse Andy Warhol, wandering through the Piazza Navona. He wandered through the crowd like a frail ghost, licking his gelato.

My biggest thrill in Rome happened quite by accident. One day I wandered down in the vast caverns and banquet halls of the Rome Hilton. The hall I wandered in had to have been taken over by a movie crew—the cables were the giveaway.

To my shock and surprise the movie being filmed starred Elizabeth Taylor, who went quietly about doing her job and making no difficulties for anybody, that I could see.

I was not to see her again until I happened to sit behind her at a rehearsal for some big special in the Kennedy Center.

She was married at the time of the special to Senator John Warner of Virginia, a union that didn't last. She had, as I have said elsewhere, extremely beautiful eyes. (Out of loyalty to Irving Lazar as he was dying, she came to his last Oscar party; during the Oscar ceremony Taylor had made a very fine speech about the need for more money for AIDS research. The writer Harold Brodkey, who was at the time dying of the disease, was at our table when she spoke and was visibly moved. She came over to our table and I thanked her, frankly dazzled by those remarkable eyes.)

Daisy Miller did not exactly rock the box offices of the world, but it did respectably, and was, in my opinion, respectable as a film. Since Peter had just made three big hits the studios were ready enough to allow him this star-making effort.

My son whiled away the long Swiss evenings by playing foosball with the future producer Frank Marshall and other members of the crew.

Once the movie wrapped there was a sad note. The young actor Barry Brown, who played Daisy's none too active suitor, was found dead in his car on a New York street. I didn't know him well, but I did see in him a kind of self-disappointment—perfect for that role but not so perfect for life. It was a look compounded of fear and emptiness—many actors have it when they are not playing a part.

17

I RETURNED FROM Switzerland bringing with me a very disorderly man-uscript—the disorder was the result of my writing half on Swiss, half on Italian typewriters. This was a novel called *Terms of Endearment*—for long my favorite among my many fictions. I have come to like a later book, *Duane's Depressed,* just as much and maybe more, but *Terms of En-dearment* still seems like my most mature fiction. It's the story of a mother and a daughter, a subject that has always fascinated me. And *Terms* is the ripest fruit of this fascination, although the little-read *Loop Group* is also pretty good on mothers and their girls.

The long-sustained interest in *Terms* in Hollywood has some curious aspects, though. Aurora Greenway, played memorably in the film by Shirley MacLaine, sort of took over the book and would have taken over the movie had not Debra Winger thrown up a formidable barrier.

Emma Horton, the Winger role, turned out to be a character I no lon-ger really owned. Long ago she was sold along with all the characters in *All My Friends Are Going to Be Strangers* to an insurance man in New York—I was so green in the early 70s that I failed to protect any of my characters for future use. (To this day Sony owns most of the characters in the *Last Picture Show* quintet.)

Fortunately, when I made the sale of *All My Friends* I did have enough sense to keep some profit points for myself. These were pretty much worthless until a successful film was actually made, but they could be used to lure investors, which is what Elliott Coulter, the insurance man, mainly did with them.

In time I traded all my points in order to retain my favorite character, Emma Horton. I've never regretted it. Had I not made this trade, *Terms of Endearment* would likely not have been made.

The sets, I am told, were already being struck when Jack Nicholson decided to gamble and play the astronaut (in the book he is merely a general, retired).

Raising even the modest amount of money it took to make *Terms* was not easily accomplished, mainly because the heroine was a middle-aged woman. At the time Barbra Streisand was about the only female star who could get a movie made pretty much on demand.

Women who can carry a feature film are rare in any market. Julia Roberts is currently one who can—but even she only has a few years of such power left.

Before the movie was green-lighted there was one woman with a deep interest in playing Aurora, and that was Jennifer Jones, then married to the very rich art collector Norton Simon. Jennifer Jones, widow of David O. Selznick, knew a few things about Hollywood and used all her savvy to advance her candidacy for the role of Aurora.

I would have been fine with Jennifer Jones, though she did not have quite the bite Shirley MacLaine can muster.

Rich as she was, when Jennifer Jones set out to try and capture the role of Aurora she really had only one ace in her deck, and that was her long friendship with Cary Grant. If only Cary Grant had wanted to come out of retirement and play the general, the movie would likely have been made, pronto.

But woe: Cary Grant declined, at which point Jennifer Jones quietly folded her hand; she offered her option to director James L. Brooks, the powerful TV producer who had done *The Mary Tyler Moore Show* and also *Taxi*.

Before this rejection Jennifer Jones staged a dinner, mainly in order to convince me what a wonderful Aurora she would be. Marcia Carter and I were in town for a book fair and agreed to come to the dinner in Malibu, where the Simons owned adjacent houses: one for them and one for his art (the same arrangement that Averell Harriman had in Georgetown).

When we reached Malibu we were told that Norton Simon was returning from a far place and would be a little late. We sat at a table that was no more than five feet above the Pacific: this was as close as I had been to the great water until, decades later, I took a trip to French Polynesia.

Jennifer Jones arrived, dressed in dramatic black, and a bit décolleté. Then Norton Simon himself popped in—he soon rushed Marcia off to the other house, to show her his art collection, now mostly in a museum in Pasadena. The food was good. Gauchely, I almost mistook carafes of oil and vinegar for white wine, but I woke up just in time.

I would have loved to have had Jennifer Jones play Aurora, but I knew at once that it was not to be. Once the project passed to James L. Brooks, he had no easy time getting it made. Diane Keaton, the original Emma, gave way to Barbara Harris and several others. Fortunately just then, *Urban Cowboy* came along and Debra Winger took the role. She gave a wonderful performance as Emma, the character who had stayed with me for ten years and I still miss, in that strange way that novelists miss their own creations.

Once he had a solid grip on the rights to *Terms of Endearment,* James Brooks paid me a courtesy call in D.C. He wanted to explain what he planned to do with my book. I knew he would have to get a bankable male into the cast, and, in my opinion, turning the brusque old general into an astronaut seemed the perfect solution. I heard they were considering

Robert Duvall, who, fine actor as he is, probably couldn't have brought in quite enough money. For that you need stars, and Duvall wasn't one yet.

What James Brooks had the courtesy to come and tell me was that he had in mind to make a kind of parallel story to my own. The emotional thread between Emma and Aurora would remain. This sounded smart to me—I raised no objection. In the film the story only slants back toward my story as Emma is dying.

With or without my good opinion the film remained a hard make. James Brooks circled the studios a couple of times, looking for money. He had to chip in a bit of his own to seal the deal. Meanwhile Shirley MacLaine waited and waited, and was awarded with an Oscar for her patience.

Had Jack Nicholson not made the last-minute decision to come in as the astronaut, I still doubt that the film would have been made, and he did take a gamble: it's rare for a star of his magnitude to take a role in which he is only on the screen some 20 percent of the time, instead of the 80 percent many stars demand and get. Jack Nicholson brought a quality of ebullience to the role, a quality the film really had to have.

The picture, when finally made, reaped a bumper crop of Oscars, including best picture, a triumph Paramount, which had never been happy with the picture, must have been very happy with.

18

My hotel in Hollywood became, for a time, the Chateau Marmont. Somebody told me writers stayed there, and once I believed them. At least one other writer stayed there, Renata Adler, who wrote about it in *A Year in the Dark*.

I had trouble with the Chateau's labyrinthine basement and parking garage, which presented one with a maze of pillars. During my time at the Chateau if there were other writers staying there, they must have been invisible, because I never saw a one.

My first Hollywood novel, *Somebody's Darling*, came to me as a small gift from the gods. I was leaving Peter's office at Columbia when I heard what sounded like a slap; then a young woman in a T-shirt burst out of the doorway right beside me. She was in tears, copious tears.

"Come back, you no-talent bitch," a voice said, from inside the door. The man who had just slapped the young woman stuck his head out, saw me—I was momentarily frozen in place—then he shut the door and I never saw either the man or the young woman again. But I used her in *All My Friends Are Going to Be Strangers* as a fairly minor character, just as I had used Aurora Greenway—using her in *Terms*, as well as the ghastly *Evening Star*.

I knew, as I was writing *All My Friends*, that I would come back to the young woman who had been slapped. Her name became Jill Peel. And I did use her, in *Somebody's Darling,* in which book I went back to the three-voice method of *Leaving Cheyenne:* I allowed three major characters in the book to tell the story as they saw it, in their own voices.

By the time of *Somebody's Darling* I had been working in Hollywood nearly twenty years and I still didn't know enough about the town to write a wholly convincing book about it. The book has its moments, but these are scattered; the recollections of the old screenwriter Joe Percy are my favorite parts, now that I too, like Joe, have become an old screenwriter.

My other Hollywood novel, *Loop Group,* though wholly ignored, contains a far better picture of what one might call working-girl Hollywood, about which, by gosh and by golly, I finally began to learn a few things.

On the other hand, *Somebody's Darling* brought a permanent friend, the incandescently lovely Diane Keaton, into my life. She and I started working on this friendship in 1980 and it has, over time, borne a rich fruit. I am also permanent friends with her sister, Dorrie Hall, dealer in many interesting *objets,* mainly Western.

What we *didn't* do, along the way, was get *Somebody's Darling* filmed. The story, like *Loop Group,* had the misfortune of being *about* Hollywood, and it's a Hollywood truism that movies about Hollywood never make money.

Probably Hollywood exists to *create* illusions, not dispel them, which even a low-wattage story such as *Somebody's Darling* might tend to do. The dream factory just can't afford to dream about itself.

Diane Keaton didn't get to play Jill Peel, or Emma in *Terms of Endearment,* or (so far) Maggie in *Loop Group,* but I'm still hoping to tempt her with the role of K. K. Slater in *Rhino Ranch.* Why? K.K. is a billionairess, and I'm certain that Diane would not be averse to having billions of dollars, even if it was play money.

19

ONCE I STARTED staying at the Beverly Wilshire—now the Regent Beverly Wilshire—I started seeing the kinds of people you were supposed to meet in Hollywood. I stepped into an elevator and there were Mel Tillis and Muhammad Ali. On another visit I saw the Prince of Wales, looking nervous as he waited for his car; the then owner of the Beverly Wilshire, Don Hernando Courtright, had housed his share of royalty and was trying to soothe the nervous Prince, but I don't believe he was getting anywhere. Prince Charles is probably always nervous.

In the 70s and 80s the Beverly Wilshire had probably the best coffee shop in Hollywood, the Cafe of the Pink Turtle, whose counterman at the time I think was named Mike, though I'm not sure. Mike was the best counterman bar none I've ever met. At the Cafe of the Pink Turtle the action was always fast and furious, mainly because all three of the major talent agencies were nearby. ICM down the street, CAA up the street, and William Morris just out the back door. All those agents needed a little protein before launching into deal making. Mike and the other counterpeople fed them quickly and well and sent them out into the world of sham and hype.

Now and then Mr. Zeppo Marx, who lived upstairs, would creep into a corner booth and at once be served. On what I believe was his last birthday, in 1979, they baked him a birthday cake and sang "Happy Birthday." I was touched and so were all the other customers.

In the 80s, when I was working mostly in the Valley, I bowed to economic necessity and rented half a house, on Ranchito Street, not far from Warners and Universal. The ever-tightening traffic was an element in my decision. Getting over Coldwater Canyon to the Beverly Wilshire, where rooms cost a small fortune anyway, was beginning to overwhelm me.

By staying in the Valley I had more reason to get in to (or on to) the Universal lot—for some reason I never feel welcome at the Universal gates, as I've written elsewhere. Getting on that lot has long been the hardest part of screenwriting. To this day I don't know why.

My half of the house on Ranchito was spacious and had a pool, but I rarely swim. After a few years my son and his band sometimes stayed there; in the end my heart still belonged to the Beverly Wilshire where I stay now.

Hollywooders with long memories probably remember that the now very domestic Warren Beatty once had the penthouse of the Beverly Wilshire, a bachelor pad for the ages, which had a couch in it on which so many scripts got piled that the poor couch broke down. In the same penthouse, legend had it, occurred numberless seductions.

I never expected to see, much less stay in, this legendary place, but it so happened I did, twice. I arrived late at the Wilshire once to find a *protest* going on. A *protest*? At the Wilshire? At midnight?

Turns out that the protest was against the then president of Romania—not the tyrant Ceaușescu—who was in town trying to promote a Romanian mineral water, gallons of which were available all over the hotel. The famous Beatty penthouse was on the tenth floor, two floors above where the elevator stopped, which was at eight, the presidental suite. I was toting my typewriter, at which the president's security cast a wary eye; but they let me pass. There was a moment of awkwardness and I was allowed to go on up. Typewriters, after all, were still more common in Romania than, by that time, they were in Los Angeles.

Despite the protest far below I slept so soundly in the Warren Beatty suite that the next time I had to stay overnight in Los Angeles I booked the suite for myself—and not a word was said.

It was not particularly stylish or glamorous but I'd have to say that you can't beat it for handy.

Once I dined with Warren Beatty during a period when he was thinking of making a movie about an evangelist. I had once written a script about the famous Billy Sunday, a fact which drew from my host more questions than I have ever been asked by anyone at a single sitting.

So far Warren Beatty has not, to my knowledge, made a movie about an evangelist, but he's still got plenty of time.

20

ONE THING THAT continues to amaze me about the movie business is the haphazard way people in it go about hiring screenwriters. A particularly intriguing aspect of this practice is the hiring of scriptwriters who have not the slightest intellectual or emotional link to the project in question. I don't think there are many screenwriters who are qualified to write a script about just anything. Eric Roth, who adapted *Forrest Gump,* can do certain things, Diana and I can do some things, but none of the above can successfully do just *any* old thing.

Well, I should add that they *could* do certain things if they don't mind being silly; most of us resist pure silliness until the bills pile up on the floor. It should be mentioned that about 95 percent of screenwriting is journeyman work. Now and then some lucky screenwriter may stumble onto a project that offers the possibility of becoming art. Some of Woody Allen's many films are, and probably a few great directors—Kubrick, maybe—could do it, but only if their writers are good enough to do it on their own, at least occasionally. Why, to quote an old example, did Howard Hawks use William Faulkner as one of the writers on *Land of the Pharaohs*? How much could William Faulkner have known about Egypt during the time of the pharaohs? Faulkner, by this time, had already won the Nobel Prize. Why would he have gone to

Hollywood to write a movie that he must have known would be pretty silly?

I'll take the questions in order. Probably Hawks thought of Faulkner because he knew him, liked him, and knew he could do reliable hackwork. He could be trusted to do a competent job.

Why Faulkner took the job, having pocketed his Nobel Prize money, may have been because he was already broke. Did he feel he owed Howard Hawks a favor for work supplied when Faulkner needed money? (I wrote a couple of scripts for the producer Martin Starger because he had previously given me jobs when I needed them.)

In Faulkner's case there was the additional lure of Meta Carpenter, his longtime Hollywood girlfriend, who was to write a lovely book about him called *A Loving Gentleman*.

Meta Carpenter was a true Hollywood working girl, of the sort I wrote about in *Loop Group*. I had hoped to meet her on the set—or at least in the vicinity—of *Terms of Endearment* when they were shooting in Nebraska. The meeting didn't happen because she got fired that day. Kristi Zea, the costumer, was to dine with her, but she left and Kristi and I dined alone.

21

AT SOME POINT in time most Hollywood writers get ahead, but they are often not able to stay ahead. Even fewer of the crew members manage to stay ahead. Meta Carpenter did what was called "holding script": guarding against inconsistencies of dress from setup to setup, which took a steady and retentive eye.

As for staying ahead, both S. J. Perelman and Anita Loos have remarked about how sizable sums of money just seem to melt when you try to take it out of the Los Angeles Basin. I've experienced this odd melting process myself.

For most of the 80s, as I said, I mainly worked on the Warners/Universal side of the hill. My bibliophilic mainstay in those years was Dutton's bookshop on Laurel Canyon at Magnolia. They also had a good store in Brentwood; both are now closed. In fact I was making a speech at the downtown Public Library at the very moment the Brentwood Dutton's closed.

At one point the Dutton's on Laurel was kept so busy buying books out of passing cars that they had a full-time buyer in the parking lot. Many a day, while enduring a tedious story conference, I spent my time daydreaming about what I would be buying if I were on assignment in the Dutton's parking lot that day.

22

THERE WAS IN England at that time a former hoofer named Lew Grade—
he came from somewhere in Central Europe and in the trade was instantly
dubbed Lord Low Grade, because of the terrible but popular television
fare he dished up to the English.

Lord Grade, inevitably, sought to broaden his horizons, that is, to
come to America and make feature films. He promptly formed a company called Marble Arch and hired a friend of mine, the producer Martin
Starger, to run it. Marty had once been a power at ABC and was probably
ready for a less exhausting job.

Martin Starger took Lord Grade's offer and soon found himself in a
mini–Marble Arch just off Ventura Boulevard, in the heart of the Valley.
He at once began to make movies from the properties Lew Grade had acquired, one of which was the wildly popular techno-thriller named *Raise
the Titanic!* What he failed to notice when he optioned the book was that
it was less a novel than a manual on how to raise a very large boat from
deep beneath the sea.

I didn't like the book, but I did like Martin Starger and agreed to give
the project a whirl. I was later to discover that around seventeen writers had
made the same decision. (I was the only one who didn't petition for credit.)

To impress me with the seriousness of Marble Arch's determination,

Marty took me down to the lab, where a lot of techs in white coats were peering at the huge—fifty-five feet—model of the *Titanic,* which was on a large table. The engineers were discussing the degree of oxidation that must have occurred while the boat was in the water.

I had no opinion as to the degree of oxidation so we went to lunch.

The model would eventually be shipped to Malta, where there was a big sea tank, the nautical location of choice for movies requiring battles on the high seas.

That was all fine with me, but it didn't answer or even ask the myriad of questions about how to adapt the book into a halfway watchable movie. This question never got delved into very deeply, though the film got made by hook and by crook; it starred Jason Robards, who wasn't good but then if he had been it would would have been a miracle.

I tried to sell Marty and company on Howard Hughes and the *Glomar* story as a possible way out, but as we were scripting it a novel was published so close to our subject matter that I just let it go.

The *Glomar* story involved the Russian submarine *K-129,* which sank with many doomed sailors and some valuable codebooks inside it. Howard Hughes designed the *Glomar* to raise the sub, even giving the Russian sailors a proper Russian burial at sea. His ship is now mainly used for oil exploration, I believe, much of it for Russia.

When Lew Grade bought *Raise the Titanic!* he probably read no further in it than the cover. Where there was just a boat, he saw *Moby-Dick.* But, unfortunately, Clive Cussler isn't Melville.

For both Lew Grade and Martin Starger the worst was to come. They then made a movie called *The Legend of the Lone Ranger.* There was already an excellent script, written by George MacDonald Fraser, author of the Flashman series, upon which I did not improve. Instead I drifted out of that job and just in time too, because a public relations storm was about to break. The original Lone Ranger, of course, had been Clayton

Moore. By this time interest in the Lone Ranger had faded considerably, but Clayton Moore still made a little money opening supermarkets and other modest celebrations. His selling point was his Lone Ranger mask, which Marble Arch forced him to relinquish, thereby infuriating thousands of Lone Ranger fans who were thus deprived of the only reason they might have to go actually *see* the film. Clayton Moore lost work, though I think a deal was finally worked out. Besides, who is going to dress up silly and open supermarkets if not Clayton Moore?

From Martin Starger's point of view it became a nightmare. The film also lost lots of money; so far as I know that was the end of the story of Lord Grade's Marble Arch, American-style.

23

MARTIN STARGER SETTLED in as an independent producer at Universal, a slowdown for me since it meant getting through the always resistant gate. My solution in later years was to secure a limo driver named Reno, who was not as sinister as his name sounds, but still did a much better job of getting me on the lot than I could do myself.

Reno's other main customer was Jean-Claude Van Damme. Reno, like many experienced drivers, never used the freeways. He made his way around smoothly and quickly on secondary roads.

After the classic weak start with *Raise the Titanic!* I quickly did two much better scripts, one about the great French tightrope walker Blondin, who walked across Niagara Falls many times, even carrying people across or having lunch on his wire above the Falls. (The lunch was self-provided.) Huge bets were placed on him and the gambling crowd made several not exactly legal efforts to shake him off.

Blondin, however, didn't fall; the movie would have been fun to do, but Marty could never quite get it off.

The second good script I did with Martin Starger told the tragic story of Ed Cantrell, who died not long ago. He was a Wyoming lawman during the wildest days of the oil shale boom around Rock Springs, a community that's more than violent enough; and he shot and killed his own deputy and, to a small degree, surrogate son. The deputy was from Brooklyn and was Michael Rosa, young and not possessed of a particularly good disposition. There were two other officers in the police car when Ed shot Rosa, but neither saw the shooting. One was writing on a clipboard and the other was watching a fistfight in the parking lot of the big Western saloon.

With the help of the well-known Wyoming lawyer Gerry Spence, a jury eventually concluded that Ed acted in self-defense. Ed, though acquitted, was not redeemed. He lived out his lonely days as a sheep detective on the bleak Wyoming-Montana border.

Because the shooting in the police car produced four points of view it is possible to take it as an American *Rashomon* story—for years I hoped Warner Bros., which owns it, would give it a green light, but they haven't, and the main reason is that Gerry Spence, Ed's savior, is so convinced he is a movie actor that he threw up obstacle after obstacle in pursuit of the role. More than twenty years have passed but there is no sign that Spence has given up, despite the fact that Marty Starger long since acquired the film rights to Gerry's book, *Gunning for Justice,* which was the best account of the Cantrell tragedy (for it was no less); Starger has also purchased several articles and references to the case, but all to no avail. Spence has no real rights—never did—but he is a powerful lawyer and he would, as the studio well knows, cast ever more imaginative spanners into the works.

We had in mind Robert Redford for the Cantrell role, and Redford carried around the notion that he might do it in his hip pocket, as it were, for several years.

At some point in the proceedings Warners went to the trouble to send me to visit Spence in Jackson Hole, where he owned an expensive, showy house with the famous *Shane* view of the Grand Tetons out his window, or at least out the window of his gazebo, where he could occasionally be found composing . . . composing . . . I know not. Maybe poetry, maybe gibberish.

Anyway I was sent ahead of a whole Warner Bros. war party—all of us there to persuade Spence not to play himself.

Very quickly I learned the unlikeliness of Gerry Spence changing his mind. After being shown his closetful of fringed jackets I was required to lie on his huge bed, above which was a large TV. On it Gerry caused to be played his large collection of lawyer seminars—trial trials, more or less. They were awful. Gerry Spence has the screen presence of a noodle. He would stop dead any film he was cast in.

Nonetheless, a Learjet full of emissaries from Burbank duly arrived, and made obeisance. I got there first. Gerry was writing I know not what; and he didn't so much as glance at me. Then the whole Warners brain trust landed, my old producer friend Leslie Morgan among them. Marty Starger came, and several others. Gerry finished whatever he was composing and did his best to be gracious. We met Mrs. Spence and also Spence *minor*, Gerry's son.

Needless to say, Gerry did not waver in his determination to play himself; still hasn't. Marlon Brando was offered, but Gerry merely returned a scornful look.

The jet flew back to Burbank, and I drove off across the bleak, wintry Bridger Plateau. Only the Oklahoma Panhandle at dusk can challenge the Bridger Plateau for bleakness at winter's dusk.

Every few years some intern will troll through the Warners vaults and come upon the Cantrell script, which they will then ponder for a few days. I reminded them of it a few years ago and again they pondered and passed. I have heard that Tommy Lee Jones once considered the Cantrell script for a time. He would have been Cantrell, had anything come of this pondering. We never heard from Tommy Lee directly but someone told me he thought the trail scenes too long. I hope he runs into Gerry Spence sometime and tries him on that line.

*   *   *

I think often of the tragic fate of Ed Cantrell. We had used him twice in miniseries and liked him very much. He stayed in my ranch house for a bit, hunting wild pigs with a friend who lived nearby. He was the real-life version of Gregory Peck in the grim little black-and-white masterpiece, *The Gunfighter*. Except for that fatal night, such was Ed's reputation that he had never had to draw his gun in the line of duty, though I believe he helped recapture two killers by shooting them in the leg with a rifle. His very skill went unchallenged until Michael Rosa looked at Ed across a car seat and prompted Ed to shoot him right between his eyes.

Ed had a deep Western voice that seemed to come from the depths of his being. We used him as security on one movie—or as firearm adviser or something, to get him a little money. He met the famous Texas Ranger Joaquin Jackson and that went very well.

Ed is gone now, and that's that. Spence is still Spence.

I hear that Gerry Spence now has another huge house. It would be like him not to stop at one. I think he did a very good job in saving Ed Cantrell, because the conflict between Ed and Rosa was going to turn violent sooner or later. Rosa would not shut up and Ed would not back down. Of course, any number of people might eventually have killed Rosa, or Ed. Wyoming is not a peaceful or a tamed place.

24

IN THE MID to late 80s I was very active as a scriptwriter; I got job after job, mainly because I priced myself at the low end of the market. I'd ask for a simple $250,000 and get it easily. I would do the traditional two drafts and a polish and trot right along to the next job.

That fun ended when I became president of the PEN American Center, then situated at Broadway and Prince in New York.

By the time my PEN job ended, in June of 1991, I was eager to do some screenwriting again. Maybe it wasn't exactly thrilling work, but I missed Hollywood and I needed the money. Also I knew how fatal it is to be away from the action in the studios, if one wanted to do film work. Out of sight out of mind was never more evident than in the hiring at the big studios.

I got on the phone and was reestablishing old ties when I went out one day and had a heart attack. I was in the middle of writing *The Evening Star* when this cardiac event occurred. *The Evening Star* was my none too good sequel to *Terms of Endearment*. I was told at once that I needed quadruple bypass surgery, and the sooner the better. What had actually failed was a tiny artery, but it was plain that several bigger guys were eager to follow suit.

I figured I could finish the novel by the beginning of December, so an operation (this was August) was scheduled for December 2, at Johns Hopkins in Baltimore.

I didn't feel bad during the end of August to the beginning of December period but I'm told by my son that I was looking very gray. Indeed he said I looked immediately better—even in the ICU after the operation my improvement was striking.

The surgery changed my life forever, and the change was noticeable immediately. I went to Arizona and stayed at the gracious Arizona Inn in Tucson, one of the best hotels in the world. (I am writing these very pages from the Arizona Inn.)

I did not yet realize that I had lapsed into a state from which I could no longer write movie scripts. I could write fiction, which doesn't really require a clear mind: it's a semivisceral experience, as I've said before. No one can write screenplays in this trancelike state. Scriptwriting requires sustained and reasoned intelligence: just the kind of intelligence you're likely not to have after being worked on by a heart surgeon.

I worked cheap, as I said, and because I worked cheap I kept getting job offers: the Roy Orbison story, for example. I knew at once that I simply couldn't do it. I listened to his music, I even visited his widow, but it was no-go. I was simply too scrambled emotionally to do the linear A to Z organized narrative that becomes a screenplay.

I was staying at the time in Tucson, in the peaceful house of Diana and Sara Ossana. I took Sara to school in the morning and that was about all I did, or could, do.

Diana is from St. Louis—she had grown up around outlaw stories. She never offered herself as a scriptwriting partner but one day an offer came along that awoke something in us both: the *Pretty Boy Floyd* story, then under option to the well-known producer Jerry Weintraub. I, in my feebleness, was about to say no, but Diana didn't let me. She wanted me to work again, and to that end quickly put together some research on Charles Arthur "Pretty Boy" Floyd.

I liked her information and told her I'd take the job if she would work with me as a full partner. (Assuming that Jerry Weintraub allowed it, which he graciously did.)

Diana and I ended up writing not only several drafts of a script about Pretty Boy, but a novel about him as well. Jerry Weintraub didn't like our script, on the (to us) odd grounds that he seemed too much of a hick. Since Pretty Boy grew up in eastern Oklahoma, in a town of less than one thousand residents, it's hard to know how he could have *escaped* being a hick; so exit Jerry Weintraub, or maybe it should be enter Larry and Diana.

From time to time we tried to snatch back that script, to no avail, though when he turned up on the award circuit for *Brokeback* Jerry remembered that he knew us and had us to breakfast, where he regaled us with several of his own adventures. He produced *Ocean's Eleven* and its sequel and was on top of the world again. He decided that *Pretty Boy* was still viable and that his good friend George Clooney should direct it.

I ran into George at the Screen Actors Guild Awards, and Diana ran into him all over the Christian world, but he did not seem to be bursting with enthusiasm where *Pretty Boy* was concerned.

So far he hasn't directed it, but you never know.

25

Irving Paul Lazar, my agent, happily took on Diana too, and as a team we began to get jobs. Not great jobs, perhaps, but jobs.

There remained the problem of my defective post-surgical brain, but Diana's wasn't post-surgical and she dug up lots of stuff that might, with careful pruning, be filmable. Moreover I liked working in partnership with beautiful smart women—I had done it already and was still doing it with Marcia Carter in the rare book business. We soon even found another Ozark story—the violent, sad story of Zeke Proctor and Ned Christie, who were more or less the last two Cherokee outlaws. Once we did a book signing for *Zeke and Ned,* and several of the people who turned up claimed kin to one or another of the outlaws.

We liked scriptwriting, even when the scripts didn't get made. Our script for *Pretty Boy* languishes in the Warners vaults, probably not far from my script of *Cantrell.*

It's been a while but there's still the chance that some powerful hand will lift them out.

26

LATELY READERS HAVE begun to complain about my short chapters, although in my opinion there is no particular reason why a chapter should be long.

Does one complain to Rimbaud because of the brevity of his verse?

In fact I am old and there are very many subjects about which I have something to say—just not much.

27

One quality great moviemakers *must* have is tenacity. Warren Beatty plugged on for ten years, putting together the deals that finally got *Reds* made. Diana spent about nine on *Brokeback Mountain*. Development time for the films made from my books averages about eight years. It's not quick work. Diana brings a real avidity and passion to her film work, whereas I mostly don't.

I sometimes think my lassitude in relation to film is—weirdly—from doing too much reviewing as a young literary man of all work. I reviewed so much fiction that I lost my passion for it, and the same might be said for movies. I once saw more than a dozen on a single weekend in Times Square. But it was writing scripts—good, bad, and indifferent—that dulled the edge of my attraction to movies. Best not to professionalize a passion, as lovers the world over have discovered when they marry and notice a cooling.

When, as the heart trauma began to recede at least a bit, I was beginning to need money, so I turned to my own most popular book, *Lonesome Dove*, and produced one sequel, *Streets of Laredo*, and two prequels (*Dead Man's Walk* and *Comanche Moon*), all of which were written as fast as I could type, as if these ghosts out of the West were faxed to me from the other me, the one who had either gone ahead or stayed behind, depending on their mood.

28

THE MAIN EXCEPTION to my Western seeking after heart surgery was *Texasville,* a sequel to *Picture Show* centered on the famous oil boom of the 70s, which described the excesses of human folly as I witnessed them in Archer City and the homes of my siblings as the irresistible notion of riches came to race through and desiccate the town, all despite that the history of booms is well known. All rational people know that booms end—they do not go rocketing on forever. Even the great investor Warren Buffett, the onetime Sage of Omaha, got caught out in the crash of the late 90s, losing some twenty-five billions, which he is already well on his way to making back.

What was different about the boom of the 70s was that my three siblings and their spouses were just of an age to be swept in, and were swept in, one by one, as were the siblings of pretty much everyone else in town.

People who were working-class—who didn't need exercise machines or personal trainers because they worked all day and were not the least interested in working on weird machines throughout the evening—suddenly began to get tennis lessons at a facility in Wichita Falls. Some of them, God help us, even began to jog. My father had just passed away but if he had been alive he would probably have died laughing at this spectacle. It was a very hot summer, with a high of 116 degrees—hot enough to call off a planned marathon. Even the newly affluent aren't crazy enough to jog at 116.

This boom soon passed and tennis faded from local view. The exercise machines ceased to get much use.

I thought the whole bust to boom and back to bust was hilarious and so described it in *Texasville*. I don't think it's much of a novel but that didn't dissuade Peter Bogdanovich from dragging himself back to Archer City to make a film from it.

Scripts of *Texasville* circulate in the rare book market but not with my name on them. I had nothing to do with the film and never visited the set. (I think Peter's assistant Iris Chester wrote most of the script.)

What Peter did in *Texasville* is make a *Picture Show* family reunion. In the Hickenlooper family reunion documentary there are some hilarious moments, my favorite being an outburst by Randy Quaid about his fantasies of finally sleeping with Cybill. I believe Timothy Bottoms said much the same. There is a clip of my mother, criticizing the vulgarisms in my profane book. But the sequence that makes the documentary nearly immortal is a talking heads scene in which Peter, Polly, and Cybill array themselves on chairs in front of the long-gone Royal Theatre, more or less like Roosevelt, Churchill, and Stalin at Yalta, and talk about their difficulties of long ago, in which Peter left Polly for Cybill, as if a movie set romance was of worldwide importance. I don't remember what Peter contributed, but I do recall that Cybill expressed no regrets. Peter was visibly startled by the remark—by this time, having had a girlfriend, Dorothy Stratten, murdered, he knew something about regrets. None of them seemed to realize that the affair of long ago and the divorce that resulted were of no interest to anyone except themselves. It *did* alter their three lives forever, but Ol' Man River, which is life, just kept rolling along.

29

My career as a screenwriter breaks easily into two parts: pre– and post–Diana Ossana.

Writing teams are nothing unusual in Hollywood. Only a few very gifted persons, Woody Allen, as I mentioned for example, can write a good movie script all by themselves. Most of us in that trade quickly discover that we need someone to bounce ideas and options off; the plot, if there is one, may unfold too slowly or too fast.

During the several years that it took me to work my way through the trauma of heart surgery, I focused on easy characters from the outlaw ranks of the Old West—Billy the Kid, for example, or Calamity Jane, who was no outlaw herself but was acquainted with a few.

Eventually we slipped off my personal reservation and adapted Frederick Manfred's *Riders of Judgment,* his story of the Johnson County War, which was filmed as a miniseries called *Johnson County War* in Canada, with Diana, overseeing. Michael Cimino had used the same story in *Heaven's Gate,* his interesting but ill-fated epic—a film so expensive to make, at least as Cimino made it, that it sort of took down the genre called Westerns for some while.

Why Westerns, a stable genre since movies began, suddenly became almost unmakable is finance. First they were cheap to make—many of

John Wayne's cost between $700,000 and $800,000, a long way from the $40 million (if that's an accurate figure) that *Heaven's Gate* cost in 1980.

My own lifetime of travel in the American West, plus the fact that I came from a generation of cattlemen, gave me a slight edge—I learned not to have scenes in my Westerns that would be prohibitively expensive. One way to achieve that was to reduce the number of animals to the lowest possible figure. Animals are well protected on movie sets, and are very expensive to use. I think they worked three sets of the famous pigs in *Lonesome Dove*, pigs who in the narrative walk all the way from Texas to Montana only to get eaten.

Lonesome Dove in particular drew upon family memory, which in my family goes back into the 1870s. I had an uncle or two in the Texas Panhandle at the time Billy the Kid was killed. And I had several uncles who worked for the legendary Panhandle cattleman Charles Goodnight, whom I used in at least four novels.

My uncles were too young to participate in that adventure, but they heard stories of Billy and told them on our front porch throughout my childhood.

Those voices swelled and swelled and became *Lonesome Dove*, the book and then the film.

But that story comes a little later.

30

THIS IS A book about Hollywood, a town that supports an ethnic group called agents. One of the best of these agents, Ron Meyer, now head of Universal—soon, I guess, to move to Comcast—the studio, that is, not Ron Meyer—once declared correctly that talent agents are mainly flesh peddlers, in which capacity they help actors get parts and writers get contracts.

When people mouth off about how Hollywood has changed I remind myself of a correspondence I once perused—in my capacity of rare book appraiser—between the great Bertolt Brecht and the legendary agent Spud Weed, who departed the hills and the valleys before I came to town.

Neither Brecht nor Spud Weed bothered with long philosophical exchanges. The letters between them—notes, really—were about deals. That is to say, money. So much for this play, this short story, this script. Neither man wasted words—three sentences was a long letter for Spud Weed, and Brecht was not much more voluble. He said take it or he said leave it and that was that.

In the course of my long years in Hollywood I've found friendships with agents to be a sometimes thing. Long ago I had an agent named Evarts Ziegler, a very elegant man who had been, I think, to Princeton. He was said to prefer to represent Princetonians, which left him with James Stewart and not much of anybody else. I got along well with Mr. Ziegler, and this despite the fact that I hadn't been to Princeton. I don't remember our parting—at some point Evarts Ziegler just drifted away.

I was never a client of H. N. Swanson either. Swanie was an old gentleman who overlapped with Spud Weed, though not with myself. At various times I've toured the three major agencies: William Morris, ICM, and CAA, and have been a client of two of the three, though never a particularly happy client. Probably that was because I was a writer and writers are always small potatoes at the big agencies, particularly in the budgetary sense. They want Tom Cruise, Tom Hanks, Julia Roberts, George Clooney, Brad Pitt, and the like. You can't blame the agencies for that: after all, they are in business to make money. Spud Weed knew that, and so did Brecht.

I'm a normal screenwriter; I like to be paid a goodly sum for my efforts. But I'm also atypical, in that I like human color—even when I wasn't earning handsome monies I have often enjoyed Hollywood for the color. Lunching outside on Santa Monica Boulevard I used to see two little men drive by in a big yellow shoe. I assume they were cobblers and the yellow shoe their means of advertising that fact. I also glimpsed them once or twice in the Valley, tooling along Ventura Boulevard.

A town where men can drive around in yellow shoes is just my kind of town, I guess. If more agents drove around in shoes I might find them more likable but I'm afraid that won't happen soon.

31

FROM THE TIME I signed with Dorothea Oppenheimer as my literary agent—she took me on in the early 60s until her death from pancreatic cancer in the mid-80s—Dorothea made periodic stabs at being a movie agent, at first farming work out to Helen Strauss at the William Morris Agency, whose famous mail room has given many future movers and shakers their start: Michael Ovitz and Barry Diller, to name just two.

Helen Strauss at once concluded accurately that I wasn't worth the trouble, so Dorothea was left to market me herself. Much as I loved her—and I did love her—I knew at once that this wasn't going to work. She remained to the end a high-born Mitteleuropa woman; such movie deals as she made for me then had a disturbing habit of getting lost in translation.

For a time I made the deals myself and attempted to translate them for Dorothea, but it seldom worked smoothly. She just didn't get Hollywood and, for that matter, Hollywood didn't get her, despite all the émigrés who lived there. At some point I took over all the Hollywood deals, though she remained my literary agent until she died.

As she was dying a man who shared many of her tastes and attitudes, and was in fact her near contemporary, agewise, kindly took over much of her work. This of course was Irving Paul "Swifty" Lazar, the man who famously snatched a check from Richard Nixon's hand. Irving, as most people called him, did become my agent when Dorothea died.

Irving Lazar was a very short Jewish man from Brooklyn, the very short Jewish family of whom most of us who knew him only met on the day of his memorial service in Westwood—in fact in the famous cemetery where Marilyn Monroe and numerous other stars are buried. Wooing the great and famous was really Irving's business; it was fitting that he made himself famous enough to be buried among them.

At the very end he became delusional, and very hard to reach.

I have always been attracted to self-invented people: Susan Sontag, for example. Irving was nothing if not self-invented. He used English tailors, English shoemakers, and rode with any English who would loan him a horse. He was one of several people I know who for some reason chose to invent themselves as English gentlemen instead of Jews from Brooklyn or where- and whatever.

Irving, despite his English tailoring and his fondness for Claridge's Hotel, never became an English gentleman, but he did make himself an accepted member of what might still be called café society. At Claridge's he stayed in the cork-paneled suite usually reserved for the King of Spain. He had an apartment on Fifth Avenue and a home in Beverly Hills. Like Proust he had an acute sense of social position. I took Irving and his wife, Mary, to lunch at Petrossian, the famous caviar house whose first home was in Paris and whose New York branch was at 58th Street and Seventh Avenue.

Before he even seated himself Irving scanned the restaurant and said immediately that there was not a bad table in the house.

To the end of his days Irving made sure that he was at a good table—with a car waiting, or sometimes a plane. He had a germ phobia and was the cleanest person you were ever likely to see.

Once Diana and her daughter, Sara Ossana, passed through London on their way to Italy. I was there making a speech for PEN at the Queen's Hall, I believe.

Once I got the Ossanas settled I called Irving, who invited us over for a drink. Sara, who was traveling to Europe for the first time, had given herself a smashing haircut for the occasion. Sara's haircut made such a hit with the Lazars that they decided to ditch their dinner with the Queen of England and the King of Greece—or so Irving declared.

"Oh, we see these royals all the time," Irving claimed in the main dining room of Claridge's. "Let's just eat here." And so we did, with Irving at his most demanding. He kept snapping his fingers at the captain, ordering yet another bottle of Cristal.

He and Mary remained friends with Diana and Sara for the rest of their lives.

32

IRVING SECURED ME as a client just at the right time, in fact making the publishing deal for *Lonesome Dove* just as Dorothea was fading away.

It would be nice to say that Irving was a superb agent, but that would be far from the truth. He had deals in place with many publishers which allowed him to get his 10 percent immediately, whereas his client's payouts might be spread over years.

In my case, particularly, his carelessness cost me millions. Though he always claimed to be a lawyer, in fact law bored him. Thus when Quintex, the multinational that initially set up the *Lonesome Dove* deal, went bankrupt, Irving did not bother to follow the proceedings, costing me millions in royalties. And the money stream that is *Lonesome Dove* is still flowing now.

I figure Irving Lazar cost me at least $15 million, a sum that would always be useful. But I loved him anyway and so did many others.

33

IRVING LAZAR'S END was so Hollywood as to be almost unbelievable. All of us knew how vital Mary Lazar was to Irving's equilibrium; but not everyone expected him to go as totally out to sea as he went when Mary was discovered to have a very advanced cancer. Her death was a blow from which Irving could not recover.

By this time Irving had, among other problems, gangrene, thanks to his refusal to give up his tight, handmade English shoes. And, because he took too much morphine over too long a time, his kidneys were shutting down.

Irving knew perfectly well that his end was near, and, because of the absence of Mary, I don't think he much cared. Soon his old crony, the record producer Ahmet Ertegun, found him a companion, a woman named Teresa, who did her best to clone Mary, an effort that was doomed from the start. Agent-wise, by this time, Irving had slipped his tether. He called me often to announce wild deals, all of them totaling millions, none of which happened. He was saved from professional disgrace only by the extraordinary efforts of his assistant, Cindy Cassel, a wonderful young woman.

At some point about a month from the end Irving began to give things away, behavior that did not please Teresa. He called one day and asked if Diana and Sara would come over for a day: he wanted to give them his silver and his china. We said, of course. But when we arrived complications arose. Irving, dressed in a nice sailor suit, greeted us happily. But when we started to pack up the stuff Teresa led us into another room and told us Irving had already given the silver and the china to Lauren Bacall.

At this juncture a maid who didn't much like Teresa scuttled off and returned with a case of elegant Danish silver: it was Irving's bachelor silver, from the heady days when he shared a house with Humphrey Bogart and Frank Sinatra. It was very good silver—Diana has it still.

That evening, having our last meal at Spago, Irving asked sadly why we hadn't taken more stuff. When Diana explained that Teresa had forbidden us to, Irving gave Teresa a look that implied slow strangulation down the road.

As his days as an agent dwindled, his delusions expanded. Once he told me that he had sold one of the *Lonesome Dove* prequels to Robert Halmi Sr. for $5 million, such happy news that I dashed off a letter to Senior, as the old rogue was called; he was at his estate in Kenya, where he probably came close to dying of shock. No such sale had occurred.

Irving made more and more erratic calls, some of them to Dick Snyder, then head of Simon & Schuster, my publishers. By this time we had protected ourselves by hiring a couple of discreet lawyers, Robert Thorne and Greg Redlitz, to cautiously look over the deals Irving was claiming, just to be sure nothing illegal was happening. Nothing was, but the situation remained dicey for as long as Irving was alive.

After the incident with Robert Halmi Sr., we decided to fire Irving, or, better yet, persuade him to resign.

So, on one joyless Saturday, I journeyed for the last time up Coldwater Canyon to Irving's house. Teresa was somewhere in the house, perhaps listening on an intercom. But, fortunately, Cindy Cassel was there, helping us persuade Irving to see the light, or listen to reason, or something.

The light within Irving was dying rapidly, and we had no success. He bluntly denied that his agenting skills were slipping. He denied that he forgot deals or was in any way impaired. He had gangrene in both feet by this time, but refused to talk about it.

The day wore on rather pointlessly, until it was time for dinner, which we had at Chasen's; it was to be the last time I dined at that famous eatery, now gone. Irving had to be wheeled in in a chair, because of his swollen feet; he was in tennis shoes. Almost immediately he started a quarrel with the waiter and the quarrel ran on none too quietly throughout the dinner. The waiter, who had long ago bartended at some of Irving's wild bacchanalia, gave little ground. He jocularly threatened Irving with many shocking revelations but Irving continued to abuse him anyway.

Finally he settled down and informed me that he was giving me his Matisse—a very crude sketch but still a Matisse. While Irving was quarreling with the waiter Cindy informed me that he had given the Matisse to Gregory Peck—and only the night before. When Cindy reminded him of this he said he'd give me his Gromaire instead; but, when we got back to his house, the Gromaire was not easy to find. Eventually it was found in Mary Lazar's bedroom, hanging right over the head of a sleeping Teresa. To say that Teresa was sleeping soundly would be an understatement. The resourceful Cindy found a stepladder and lifted the picture down. I have it still.

One of my last really happy dinners with Irving had occurred in New York. I was there and he was there, but Mary Lazar was somewhere else. Irving asked if he could bring a date, a respected scientist, he emphasized.

I said sure, not knowing quite what to expect. Irving now and then visited ladies of the night. But the dinner hour came—I was treating them at Petrossian again. At the appointed time Irving waltzed in with a very beautiful young woman who *was* a respected scientist: a cancer researcher at Sloan-Kettering. She did not speak a word, and they strolled off together hand in hand. It's the way I like to remember Irving now: a small, impeccably dapper man strolling up Fifth Avenue with a beautiful young woman holding his hand.

34

Norman Mailer told me that the first time he saw Irving he was with Dorothy Parker. The last time I saw him was when he was impatiently holding a stepladder while Cindy Cassel took that picture down.

For reasons I no longer remember I was shown an inventory of Irving Lazar's estate. The first thing that struck me is that he had almost no books. He had been Nabokov's agent but there were no Nabokov books with little butterflies drawn on the fly leaves, as there were, say, in Edmund Wilson's copies.

What the inventory revealed was that Irving had spent pretty much every cent he earned on his lifestyle. He wore expensive clothes, ate at expensive restaurants, and stayed in expensive hotels—the ones a rich Englishman night stay in, if there were any.

As a country boy from Texas I naturally envied Irving's self-inventive powers—he practiced a kind of performance art that ceased to exist once the performer stopped performing. Sic transit Gloria DeHaven, as the fine, recently deceased Texas writer Edwin Shrake once quipped.

Irving vexed the Hollywood establishment agency culture, because he poached clients constantly. He was bitterly jealous of Michael Ovitz, once

Ovitz began to be dubbed the Super Agent. Irving always said that every writer had two agents, his own and Lazar. He claimed he stopped representing actors because he got tired of holding their hands. As a lone wolf he could not compete with the packaging powers of the great big agencies so he pretended they didn't exist.

35

FOR SEVERAL YEARS, in the 80s and early 90s, Irving gave his famous Oscar party at Spago, the celebrated restaurant just above Sunset Boulevard. I took Sara and Diana to the last two. At the penultimate Oscar party Mary Lazar was alive and Irving still a power: not in the studios, of course, but in the world of celebrities. To this next-to-last one Madonna came and the fact of Irving Lazar's drawing power was still obvious.

At the final Oscar party, though, the force of his social fame was abandoning Irving Paul Lazar. Mary was dead, and though the party was crowded Madonna *didn't* come. In the main only the loyalists came: Elizabeth Taylor, fresh from her moving AIDS speech on the Oscarcast. Jack Nicholson came and a few other real stars but without Madonna, the biggest star, a brightness seemed to have fallen from the air.

Sara, Diana, and myself sat at the oldies table—why waste a valuable seating on the likes of us? Opposite sat George Burns and beside us James Stewart, as silent as statues, although, as George Burns was being led out, this apparently lifeless old man winked at Sara Ossana and gave her a cigar.

That was the high moment of the evening for me. I think of it as sort of the end of the Old Hollywood, a Hollywood where stars were still more important than agents. Soon even the little men in the yellow shoe were seen on the streets no more.

The color faded out and Irving's last party began the fade.

Now I no longer see the likes of Irving Paul Lazar, whose housemate, Frank Sinatra, greatest pop singer of his era, had the grace to come to his funeral.

36

THE SECOND BOOK Diana and I were offered for scripting was a Western called *The Stand,* or *St. Agnes' Stand,* about some nuns who are trapped by Apaches in New Mexico. A Clint Eastwood–type loner shows up out of nowhere to save them but does not have complete success. I don't think we were the first writers on *The Stand* and I'm sure we weren't the last. I mention Eastwood only because of the rather similar picture, *Two Mules for Sister Sara,* in which Eastwood starred with Shirley MacLaine.

Indeed, most Westerns have at least a few similarities to other Westerns, if only because they ride horses and do whatever they do in the West.

After *The Stand* failed to attain a green light, we decided to try something a little lighter, in short to make a feature film out of the long-gone but once-popular series *Father Knows Best.* Its star, Robert Young, had passed away, and the rights at last became available. *Father Knows Best* was a good show for its era, but this is not its era. After a draft or two its producer, Sean Daniel, abruptly fired us. The man who had the task of actually doing the firing turned out to be the nephew of my old friend Joe Alsop, the acerbic columnist.

So it was goodbye, for a while, to the Universal lot.

About this time it began to strike me that the executives at the various studios where we might be hired or fired were becoming younger and younger; and more and more of them seemed to be female. At some of our meetings there would even be two females, one to be the boss and the alternate to take notes. Occasionally the alternate would be black.

Since we were mainly at the studios to pitch Westerns, it was a little disconcerting to find that the executives who were to relay our pitch had never heard of such Westerns as *The Searchers* or *Red River*.

Though we did a lot of pitching: two rounds at least at every studio, plus a number of blind stabs at likely production companies.

Very soon it became obvious to me that my name had little pull. My books had belched out several winners—*The Last Picture Show, Terms of Endearment,* and *Lonesome Dove*—but none were then *current*—and it takes little acquaintance with Hollywood to learn that *current* is critical.

By the mid-90s I was simply not *current* enough to get us even a tiny job. The entertainment industry's link to professional sports is quite obvious: an athlete is only as good as his last at-bat, his last touchdown run, etc. My own last at-bat had been, in Hollywood terms, a long time ago, even though in real time it was only maybe five years.

The heat from a hit film or series is *very* hot while it's hot, but in the experience of those who have been really hot, slack off a little and a chill will descend very quickly.

During the sad *dégringolade* of Irving Lazar we protected ourselves from his destructive caprices by hiring two crackerjack lawyers, Robert Thorne and Greg Redlitz, and we have them still. They had great respect for writers of what they called "our status," but the fact was, status or not, we counted for zilch in the world of feature films.

That being the case, the only place to go was television, which is where the two of us went next.

37

In filmmaking it is often unclear who makes the rules, and, indeed, the answer may well vary from project to project. Sometimes it's a studio head, or a studio head in tandem with a bank. Some big stars on the order of Tom Hanks may be big enough that they appear to be making the rules, but those situations are rare and brief.

With a powerful production team such as DreamWorks, with seasoned executives such as Stacey Snider steering the ship, the ship itself can be said to be making the rules; but even their power is not unlimited. DreamWorks, in its first giddy years, wanted to build a new studio in the flats by Playa del Rey; yet no studio arose.

Sharing power in order to share expenses is common in television, as well as movies; but one doesn't have to work in television very long to realize the medium really belongs to advertising. The advertisers make the rules, a point that is seldom made with much subtlety, as the great golfer Tiger Woods is now finding out. Advertising is the portal through which success or failure passes.

That's my broad-strokes point of view, formed from working mainly in television for much of the last twenty years, which is not to say that there isn't a creative infrastructure in the studios, networks, and cable that works hard to sift out a few treasures from the river of dreck that flows through Hollywood year after year. Producers and TV programmers lead very insecure lives: if one bit of programming wipes out or goes bad there goes the programmer too. Television is often close to simply running out of product, although sometimes the network heads don't see it that way.

The need to slot shows for a given age group is inhibiting to writers in ways that executives seldom seem to understand. Since Diana and I started working in television miniseries, we've worked with CBS, ABC, Fox, and HBO. We even did one nice script for Starz, but it failed to advance and has now reverted to its original owner.

The advantage we had, when we started to be TV writers, was of course *Lonesome Dove.*

There were those two prequels and one sequel, shoved into production by the success of *Lonesome Dove*. As miniseries go, ours were easy makes.

Easy, though not quick. The four films made from what turned out to be a tetralogy took twenty years. Diana Ossana was on set for the filming of three of these efforts and the solid training she got there helped make her into the extraordinary producer that she is.

38

But enough. Only the people who work in the vast chambers of the networks or cable stations really need to read anything analytical about their jobs. The fun of Hollywood—a commodity there seems to be less and less of all the time—comes from its characters, the Spud Weeds and Irving Lazars that walk its streets and frequent its expensive watering holes.

Only the people who have to deal with him regularly need to know what Leslie Moonves (head of CBS) is like or how to deal with him.

What they mainly want to know instead is what Diane Keaton or Cybill Shepherd is like; it's normal to be curious about them but they're not going to learn anything from me. Tolstoy, much provoked by his wife of forty-eight years, once said he would only tell the truth about women when he had one foot in the grave. Then, once he'd told it, he'd jump in.

The difference between Tolstoy and me is that he may actually have known the truth about women—a truth that eluded even Dr. Freud—whereas I don't.

What I do know are some funny stories about the making of movies, and these stories start with our involvement in the production of *Streets of Laredo,* which takes place near Lajitas, Texas, and other points along the Rio Grande. The stars were James Garner, Sissy Spacek, Sam Shepard, Ned Beatty, Sonia Braga, and Randy Quaid.

Streets and its prequels, of course, only got made because of the huge success of *Lonesome Dove*. I doubt that Irving, then our agent, ever read *Lonesome Dove*, but he still assessed it correctly as a potential winner. He considered several customers for the segue and settled on Suzanne De Passe, a snappy woman who was running Motown's movie wing. We had lunch at a restaurant in Hancock Park and Suzanne convinced me that a miniseries would be the way to go. To both of us it looked like *Streets of Laredo* would be television or nothing, the cost of a feature being beyond anybody's budget.

Before that happened though another colorful character entered the list, this being Robert Halmi Sr., a former photographer of whom we became rather fond.

At our first dinner with Senior, as he was called to distinguish himself from his son, Robbie, he was pissed off at me because I criticized one of the posters for the film. In fact it had my name misspelled, which Senior probably hadn't known. To demonstrate his Hungarian hauteur he ordered a $1,200 bottle of wine. (I suspect he had a deal with the sommelier, which would be like him.)

Anyway his rancor soon passed and we enjoyed a good acquaintance for several years. I like Hungarians, for example Michael Korda, my inexhaustible editor. Robert Halmi Sr. *had* to wave his saber around. Later, in D.C., I met a spy of some distinction who had known Senior in Budapest a long time ago—the 30s, I think. Many legends accrue around Robert—he even has a book about his prowess as an elephant hunter.

The pricey bottle of wine wasn't wasted, because Robert drank all of it—in time the ship sailed on and *Streets* got made; the ratings were respectable, thanks to its excellent cast.

Diana and I had met Robert one time before. The director, Joe Sargent, who had directed Ron Howard when the latter was nine (or maybe seven), was having difficulties with the fiery Sonia Braga. It was hoped that since we were writers a chat with us might calm her down. It had, of course, the reverse effect; she threw us out of her trailer, reminding us, as we were going, that writers really know very little.

Senior was around that day but made no attempt to soothe Braga. In the afternoon he flew away in a little Lear, unfortunately leaving behind the young woman he had brought with him, who was quietly returned to civilization by slower means.

We too had been brought to the set by private jet, a mode of travel I consider, as I said, to be the ultimate luxury.

There's an innate sadness on movie sets that I never fail to register. It could be, I suppose, that the sadness is in me and is merely intensified by the temporariness of a movie set, the muddle, the flimsy-seeming nature of everything that's happening.

People from many places, from homes that are stable and happy, enter a kind of purgatory, in which home rules don't apply, and where, for maybe sixty days, they joust with shadows, only a few of which you will be responsible for. The set life is composed of loneliness and muddle, relieved only now and then by flashes of brilliant work by an actor, a cameraman, a member of the crew.

I avoid sets when I can, but the one time I couldn't was when *Dead Man's Walk* was being filmed, in midwinter, again at locations around Van Horn and Alpine, both in deep West Texas.

I had to be on set because Diana couldn't, being fully engaged at the time by postproduction work on *Streets,* which was being done in L.A. I seldom expose my self to close-range postproduction. Invariably I get the unpleasant disease called mix-room pneumonia, which one is apt to get if one sits for days in a sealed room where everyone's germs have no chance to get out.

While Diana went to L.A. to deal with all that I stayed with the production team. It didn't take me long to identify the dominant feeling in a production crew: anxiety.

Crew members are anxious about getting fired, and, in fact, they often *are* fired. Directors worry about making their day: that is, shooting whatever scenes it has been decided they must shoot that day. In feature films directors often have the luxury of shooting only about a page and a half a day, which makes them the envy of television directors, who normally have to shoot five pages a day.

Actors, who work out of fear and emptiness anyway, worry about how they sound, how they look, and whether they can make their lines work.

Producers, of course, worry about when the money is going to run out, as, almost inevitably, it will at some point.

Dead Man's Walk is the first miniseries set in the time when my two famous Texas Rangers, Gus and Call, were becoming Texas Rangers. The fine English actor Jonny Lee Miller played Call, and David Arquette a wistful Gus. They lacked the weight of the older actors who had propped up *Streets of Laredo:* James Garner, Sissy Spacek, and the rest. Keith Carradine evened things up a little, and so did Edward James Olmos, Harry Dean Stanton, and Eric Schweig.

As I recall we had about a fifty-five-day shoot, much of it done close to the Rio Grande. The famous Texas Ranger Joaquin Jackson was our security man, and Ed Cantrell came down from Wyoming to play in a scene or two. Joaquin Jackson had left the Texas Rangers when they hired the first woman: the Nick Nolte movie *Extreme Prejudice* is loosely based on some of Joaquin's fearless exploits.

Two unexpected things happened during the making of *Dead Man's Walk*. One was funny and one not.

The funny one involved some Rangers who where hiding behind rocks and shooting up a hill at some Indians who were scampering around none too ominously, while firing off arrows galore at the huddled Rangers. Many of the arrows stuck in the rocks, which were of course fake. That was at least a little bit funny, though not as funny as what happened next. I was in my producer's chair, and, in order to see the ridiculous action better, I edged my chair up the hill a little too far, so that it tipped over backward and tumbled me back down the hill, where I rolled up at the feet of Robert James Waller, author of *The Bridges of Madison County,* who lived nearby. Fortunately, Mr. Waller took my little tumble in stride.

The one producer-like thing I did that was of some actual use was to prevent a bronco-busting scene that might well have cost the young Jonny Lee Miller his life. He did not ride particularly well, and in the scene as planned he would be mounting a half-broken mare only a few feet from a precipice that would have produced a very considerable fall.

This was the first scene in the book, and had been meant to establish a few things about the friendship between Gus (who's holding the mare) and Call, who was about to mount.

Thus we lost the establishing scene—I instantly canceled it—but at least we avoided getting a fine young actor hurt.

Jonny Lee was briefly married to Angelina Jolie, who auditioned for us with him. She was sullen about it, but she did it.

I also lay a small claim to having discovered the lovely Jennifer Garner, whom I spotted on a short audition tape: I knew at once that she was the girl Gus would fall in love with.

Before the filming of *Johnson County War,* which was shot in Canada, I watched, in my role as executive producer (the big cheese in TV, unlike film, where the producer is the big cheese), no fewer than one hundred and eighty audition tapes of Canadian actors giving their all in the five or six lines that had been selected to tape. What the experience taught me was to respect the desperation of actors—working, as I've already said, mainly out of fear. Watching those tapes was a Dostoyevskian experience, not one to be quickly absorbed or easily shut out of one's mind.

For lesser actors, much of their career is doing just such takes for very minimal reward.

The film had its moments but very few of the actors had theirs—mainly the star, Tom Berenger, who insisted on singing as he was being murdered. We tried to discourage him but he persuaded us and I suspect now that he was right: absurdity is better than nothing, in the movies.

39

WHEN MOVIE PROJECTS succeed—by which I mean get made—it's usually for one reason: someone connected with the project has found the money to make it. This can take a few weeks but more often takes several years. I once wrote a little script funded by the National Endowment for the Humanities, an organization that supplies a bankroll but which also comes with a complicated list of stipulations. In normal filmmaking you won't need to bother about such matters: you just have to find the money.

My NEH film was about the opposition to strip mining in Montana in the 80s. It took eighteen years to get it made, by which time I was long gone from the project, which was called *Montana* and starred Richard Crenna and Gena Rowlands.

I never saw it but understand it was pretty good. The fact that it did finally get made was because Ted Turner acquired a big ranch in Montana and was seeking tax write-offs. It began as a virtuous little film, which is possibly why I had trouble getting in sync with it. I have never, I suppose, been a particularly good citizen, especially not when citizenship interferes with the attempt to make art. *Montana* may have been the very first Turner movie—I'm not sure.

Just as films get made for complicated reasons they often don't get made for reasons just as strange. There is, for example, a script of mine called *Honkytonk Sue*—it surely rests in some archive somewhere. *Honkytonk Sue* was initially a comic strip by the brilliant Arizona cartoonist Bob Boze Bell; he has even done a graphic novel version of *Lonesome Dove*.

Honkytonk Sue was a feminist cowgirl who goes around beating up cowboys in country and western bars.

I did this script with Leslie Marmon Silko. It seemed a natural for Goldie Hawn, and we even managed to slip in London Bridge (or one of them), a segment of which spans a bit of the Colorado River at Lake Havasu City.

Leslie Silko does not easily fit in to the Hollywood way of doing things but she liked the Havasupai people and gave this one a good try. Goldie's manager at this time was a woman named Anthea Sylbert, from a family famous for its costume work in film. Anthea was a very smart woman who just happened to be somewhat at sea when it came to the interior of America.

In our climax Honkytonk Sue would occupy London Bridge and then beat the Army Corps of Engineers, who were about to flood the Havasupai, by challenging them to a massive game of bingo, in which Goldie plays about sixty competitors, among them a famous bingo fanatic from Las Vegas.

But Anthea, it turns out, had never heard of bingo. How can you be an adult in America without having heard of bingo?

That question remains unanswered, and *Honkytonk Sue* remains unmade.

40

I MET THE director Steven Spielberg only once, at a fete his company, then called Amblin, had thrown when the big American booksellers annual convention was in L.A. The party was held on the Universal lot. Diana and I were there because our novel *Pretty Boy Floyd* had just been published.

We had just started to have a word with Mr. Spielberg but didn't because the writer Jayne Anne Phillips interrupted just as Mr. Spielberg was opening his mouth to greet us.

Well, the fete was enormous and someone soon interrupted Jayne Anne Phillips too, and a pretty good time was had by all.

A few years before Diana and I became writing partners I had been invited by Amblin to attempt a script of the famous novel *The Color Purple*. Oprah Winfrey was already signed to star.

I was in the minority of readers who didn't like *The Color Purple*; I found it unappealing and, also, unconvincing. I hated the book's ending, and did not see how, for the life of me, the African stuff could be made to work.

But, since I was living in my half house in Sherman Oaks, with Universal just a stone's throw away, I accepted the meeting, though I did tell the executive in charge of the meeting that I had reservations about the job. The executive was Lucy Fisher, with whom I had had a little wrangle back on the strip mine movie. Lucy Fisher was then running the old studio in Hollywood that Francis Coppola had bought, though he lacked the money to run it.

But, no matter. I finally got paid by Zoetrope, Coppola's company, and I decided to let bygones be bygones. Besides, my old friend from *Daisy Miller*, Frank Marshall, was then, with his soon-to-be wife, Kathleen Kennedy, more or less managing Amblin while Steven Spielberg was away making movies.

In actual practice I rated that meeting as about a four on a scale of ten. The great musician Quincy Jones (who was a coproducer) was there, and Lucy, and Frank and Kathleen, and a few folks I could not quite identify.

I mentioned that I was not convinced by the book, at which heresy Quincy Jones managed to keep his cool. When I brought up the vexing matter of how to integrate the African stuff there was an awkward silence. "Oh, Steven has an idea about that," someone said. His idea seemed to involve a herd of giraffes moving across a big African sunset. How that provided the necessary link I didn't see and still don't. It didn't matter, because by that time I knew I wasn't getting the job. In stark fact, I didn't even *want* the job.

I *did* want to read Alice Walker's script, and eventually was allowed to see it, but not before the script I took home was stamped verso and recto with the Amblin symbol. That I could understand. Steven Spielberg was the most powerful director in Hollywood. Danger that he would be pirated or copied was real.

Skip ahead four years. *The Color Purple* was released to solid acclaim. It did not really rock the heavens, though it did pretty well.

In the meantime I had gotten to know Jonathan Kaplan, director of the drag racing movie *Heart Like a Wheel*, because we had worked together on a movie involving John Mellencamp.

I knew that Jonathan had just directed a film involving real, live chimpanzees; it had gone badly. The chimps ran amok—Jane Goodall could have told them about that. Several people were bitten, including, I believe, Jonathan himself.

Not long after that I was heading into the main Warner Bros. building for a meeting about something and there, sitting on the steps, was Jonathan, looking glum. When I stopped to chat he made a number of unfriendly comments about chimpanzees.

"But I did get one break," he said. "Steven Spielberg called me up and asked me to do some second unit work. We drove a big herd of giraffes across the sunset."

Thus does genius find its way, I guess. I never saw *The Color Purple,* and don't know if the herd of giraffes, aided by the sunset, straightened things out or not.

41

My LATE FRIEND Susan Sontag didn't miss much. My permanent friend Diane Keaton, nor my other permanent friend, Diane's sister, Dorrie Hall, don't miss much either. In my experience the one Hollywood figure who misses *nothing* is Barbra Streisand.

The great diarist James Lees-Milne, whose twelve-volume diary describes nearly every picky person to appear on the London social scene over more than half a century, said that Cecil Beaton, the photographer and lover of Greta Garbo, missed the least of anyone he had known, which is pretty much everybody.

Barbra Streisand is my Cecil Beaton, the host who spots the speck of potato on the chin or hairs growing out of one's nose. I once played tennis as Barbra Streisand's partner; I didn't play that badly, but so intense was her focus, so pervasive her radar, that, on the trip back to my hotel, the Chateau Marmont on this occasion, I leaned out the window of my car and vomited the whole way. Barbra had been perfectly cordial but it was still scary to play tennis with her.

It didn't help that Barbra had a French cook—after the tensions of the tennis court eating a lot of rich French sauces proved to be a bad idea.

I supply this ridiculous incident merely to show that really *big* stars—Jack Nicholson, for example—often have an impact that emanates from their fame. When the Lakers are playing at home and Jack is there in his place, all's more or less right with the world. Take away Jack and the whole of the Staples Center seems to be tipping out of balance.

This great star's mere presence has become an integral part of Lakers basketball.

Probably only a handful of the millions who have seen Jack Nicholson in that seat remember that he once directed a fine little basketball film himself: *Drive, He Said,* adapted from a novel by Jeremy Larner.

Long ago Diane Keaton and I offered him our screenplay *Somebody's Darling.* He made no response, at least to me, for more than a decade before calling me one night, out of the blue, to thank me—it was a rambling conversation, the sort at which I don't excel, as the director Ang Lee was to find out to his sorrow decades later. I believe Jack's fallen in love with my luminous friend Diane Keaton at least twice—indeed, who wouldn't? Onlookers report that Jack was extremely courtly during the making of *Something's Gotta Give,* rising when she entered, certainly a rare courtesy in Hollywood now.

Some weeks later, while she was stuck in a traffic jam, Diane called me. I've helped ease her through hundreds of traffic jams, on both coasts, for decades.

"I have issues but at least it's not boring," she said. Then the light must have changed; she hung up and I was left to wonder what the issues were.

There have been no further references to the biggest movie star who happens to live on Mulholland Drive, now that Marlon Brando has passed on.

I've rattled on about this because I find the fact of stardom itself to be interesting. My conclusion is that everyone who has a chance to be a star by all means should—but they had best go into it with their eyes open, for sooner or later stardom takes its toll. It will become like Lakers basketball *without* Jack Nicholson, the most inspired male actor of his generation, hopping around on his expensive seat.

42

THANKS TO THE fact that I've had nearly seventy jobs in Hollywood—some of them, admittedly, very small jobs: just a week here or a week there, polishing somebody else's script—I've developed a kind of Mr. Micawberish confidence that, when Diana and I need screen work, it will somehow appear. Something will always turn up.

In earlier decades I thought that I would be out of the screenwriting business before my seventies, but it hasn't turned out that way. At seventy-three, with Diana's help I'm still pecking them out. Most of what I've done is journeyman work—or at least it was until she came along.

I assumed I'd make enough writing fiction to let Hollywood go, but . . . well, I haven't. And besides the need that keeps me active in Grub Street, I *like* Hollywood too much to *want* to let it go.

I like, for example, certain semi-obscure streets, dusty little De Longpre Avenue, for example, which I have used in two novels, *Cadillac Jack* and *Loop Group*. I like the major streets too: Sunset Boulevard at dusk, Hollywood Boulevard always, though it's certainly sad that the wonderful bookshops that first brought me there are now vanished—gone. But I like Ocean Avenue too, and I like shooting the rapids in the Cahuenga Pass. Downtown L.A. is a foreign country now; when I first explored it, Dawson's bookshop was still there.

Pershing Square was then (the 60s) still pretty much as described by John Rechy in *City of Night*.

For a long time I got a little kick from having a script meeting in the Irving Thalberg Building at MGM—just, maybe, for the echoes. Somewhere in the MGM archive is one of my better early scripts, written in hope of attracting Robert Redford. It's adapted from *The Massacre at Fall Creek,* by Jessamyn West, and the real event that inspired it occurred in what is now Indiana, in 1824, up to which point it had not been a crime in America to kill Native Americans. A bunch of local racists, on what was then the very edge of the frontier, wiped out a small, poor band who were there to pick berries.

Though, as I've said, it was not a crime to kill Indians, Fall Creek aroused the great tribal powers, who threatened to set the frontier ablaze.

The powers that were in Washington did not take this threat lightly: they knew what the tribes could do. So seriously was the challenge taken that the government hastily convened a show trial—the Native leaders assembled for this trial in all their finery, and carefully observed the application of white man's law.

Three of the killers were convicted and two of them were hung. Though the Indians may not have been fully satisfied, they left the frontier unrazed. In a practical sense it remained not even a misdemeanor to kill Indians in much of the American West. The killers who were indicted in the Camp Grant Massacre numbered about one hundred, and were acquitted in nineteen minutes.

The principal producer of *Fall Creek* was the flamboyant David Merrick, who brought the English director Jack Clayton to direct; Jack was fresh from filming *The Great Gatsby* with Robert Redford as Jay Gatsby. Jack thought that if anybody could make the Indian killer sympathetic, it would be Redford. This didn't happen; Redford declined the role, though he may have sort of carried it in his head for a time, thinking that he might get around to it someday. Tom Hanks did the same with my novel *Boone's Lick,* before leaving it sit on the runway, more or less. Redford may have done the same thing with the Cantrell story. We chatted about it at a party in Austin—a big star keeping in distant touch with a project that might someday go. Clint Eastwood bought *Unforgiven* and put it in a drawer for seventeen years; then he took it out of the drawer, did it, and did it well. Very few stars are directors who can afford this kind of wait, but when they can a lovely picture often results.

43

OF THE MANY directors I've known and worked with Jack Clayton turned out to be much the most fun. He let everyone know that he had been a commando in World War II, and he exhibited his commando instincts several times while I was working with him.

As an example he stayed by choice in the Watergate Hotel, then the source of recent scandal. Naturally Jack recorded every word of his many disputes with Mr. Merrick. Since he was living on the site associated with the most famous taping in history, he couldn't resist getting his own record into history.

Jack was married to the famous Israeli movie star Haya Harareet, who had played the ingenue in *Ben-Hur*. Jack, perhaps justly, felt the world was out to get either Haya or him.

We spent our working days on *Massacre at Fall Creek* in the big room of our bookshop, and the kind of characters who happened to wander in struck Jack Clayton as deeply suspicious his first day there; often he'd get up and position himself behind them, carrying our heavy nineteenth-century milking stool—the only weaponlike instrument in the shop.

Clearly Jack Clayton had little notion of how very odd the denizens of the rare book world can be. Fortunately every customer was well behaved that day, and none of them got whacked with the milking stool, which we soon removed to the closet for the duration of my story conferences with Jack Clayton.

Unfortunately for the project David Merrick had a serious stroke and *Massacre at Fall Creek* sank out of sight.

I had one final discussion with Jack Clayton, about a book by James Kennaway, set in South Africa during a revolution—or, at least, a riot. A white man and a black man hide out together, but never speak. It's a good novel, but silence is a nonstarter in the movie business. Jack's version of *Gatsby* was not well received and I do not recall him having worked much since. Ephraim Katz's great *Film Encyclopedia* mentions two of his wives but doesn't mention Haya Harareet. Maybe she was one of the wives, perhaps even changed her name. I did see, not long ago, Jack's fine adaptation of Brian Moore's *The Lonely Passion of Judith Hearne:* Brian Moore's best work and perhaps Jack Clayton's too.

44

ONE SURE WAY to judge the relative force of books, movies, and TV is the number of impostors a given vehicle brings out of the woodwork to torment the successful creators, when they can be found.

Books, even very successful books, seldom register on what I call the Impostor Index. I don't know of many book writers who are seriously pestered by people pretending to be them. A few writers do have stalkers: I had one myself for a number of years, which is still rather different from having someone pretending to the public that they are you. This is different too from the new active crime of identity theft.

Many movie stars have stalkers, but few impostors, since the crowd at large would be so familiar with the star as to make imitation difficult. A star's looks are part of his or her currency. Woody Allen recently collected $5 million from a company that had improperly used his image, and he was right to go after them, I think.

Nowadays, though, television, not movies, is the medium with the longest reach, the solidest base. I had never lost a wink of sleep over the possibility of having an impostor, but then *Lonesome Dove* came out and all that changed. That miniseries, as I've mentioned, has been seen by over one hundred million people, I'm told, which is a lot more people than usually see most films. Films made of books by Dan Brown (*The Da Vinci*

Code) and J. K. Rowling (*Harry Potter*) have been seen by more, but those are exceptions.

Most writers have to worry that their numbers are too low—not so high that they bring out endless hordes.

The huge popularity of *Lonesome Dove* rapidly gained me at least five impostors. First came a call from a woman in Dallas who claimed that I slept with her on Thanksgiving Day—a claim easily disproved since I was with my family that day. Still, I had to hire a detective to dissuade her from this notion. The detective eventually sustained files on four different Larry McMurtry impostors, all of whom were middle-aged bullshitters, none of them attractive. One, who hailed from Green Valley, Arizona, liked to hang out at filling stations in south Tucson, attempting to entice promising girls with a part in his new film, a sequel of course to the wildly popular *Lonesome Dove*. One young lady was initially tempted but her father figured out the scam and quickly put a stop to it. This gentleman's only connection to the movies was a trained dog.

A more enterprising impostor turned up in Houston, where this person pretending to be me had conned a young lady to such a point that she was prepared to marry him. She had worked full-time at a McDonald's, supporting the man who was pretending to be me. In the mug shot my detective procured, the fellow had clearly been rather badly punched about. I got wind of the impending marriage in New York and called her mother, who did not appreciate being told that her daughter was not marrying Larry McMurtry, me, but some nameless scrounger whose driver's license she does not appear to have looked at. The mother was indignant. Indignant at my unwillingness to become their son-in-law.

At one point, as I've said, I was up to five impostors, but soon most of them began to lose steam and fade out. The one who didn't lose steam was Sam Botts. He hails, I believe, from Fort Worth, Texas; his parents are in the phone book there, and Sam began his career by pretending to be me in dinner theaters in the Dallas–Fort Worth area. Perhaps he scored a few dates by pretending to be me, but I don't know that; in any case Sam soon shifted his base of operation to the Mexican Riviera: Acapulco, Puerto Vallarta, Cabo San Lucas, and places further south. His run in Mexico lasted about a decade. He clearly had a likable side, but, unfortunately, also an unlikable side. Evidence of his likable side exists in a stream of Christmas cards from families he met, all addressed to Sam as me.

I would have liked to make a legal response to Sam, but I could not find that he had committed any crime. He carefully stayed within the limits of the law—now and then he'd get some innocent Midwesterner to cash a check for him, but they were all for small sums. One hundred dollars was about as high as he went.

Now and then he flew off the handle, threw sand at somebody, spat at the bartender, rowdiness of that sort, which, in a country where beheadings are becoming increasingly common, also did not interest the law. Copies of my books signed by someone other than me began to trickle into the L.A. market, when there was one. I was asked to rule on a few signatures, most of which I rejected, but there are plenty of forgers and I can't prove that Sam indulged in that sport.

I do understand that Sam, in his role as me, has been banned for life from the Hard Rock Cafes in both Puerto Vallarta and New York City.

Lately I have heard that Sam Botts has moved back to Texas, where he is said to be working, once again, the dinner theater circuit where he first got the idea of being me. This is a little dangerous, because quite a lot of Texans know me, and the *Dallas Morning News* went so far as to publish pictures of both of us, side by side, so patrons of the bars and honky-tonks won't be taken in, though probably some gullible folks still are.

At his best Sam Botts must have been very persuasive. When I walked into the executive air terminal at Hobby Airport in Houston to be flown back to Van Horn, where a movie crew was waiting, the two pilots who were to fly me west looked really startled when I shook their hands.

"Is something the matter?" I asked.

"It's just that you don't look like yourself," one said.

"How would you know—we've never met," I pointed out.

They looked at each other in dismay.

"Oh yes," one said. "We had drinks with you two nights ago, in Cabo San Lucas."

I told them about Sam's long-running role as my principal impostor, but I'm not sure they were entirely convinced, which is perhaps why they initially set me down in Alpine, rather than where I needed to go.

45

MOST SUCCESSFUL MOVIES become successful through a combination of luck and intent. In the case of the famous *Brokeback Mountain,* the story of two gay ranch hands who fall in love in the mostly ungay Rocky Mountains, of course there was some luck involved in its making—the luck of having Annie Proulx write a masterpiece, for example—but its making was a matter of long intent, much of which belonged to my partner, Diana Ossana, who read the story in *The New Yorker* as soon as it came out. She was visiting me in Texas at the time and I remember her racing downstairs with the magazine in her hand, demanding that I read the short story. I don't read much short fiction but I read "Brokeback Mountain" and knew at once that it was a masterpiece, and I even felt a rare stab of envy. That story had been sitting there all my life. I knew of gay cowboys; there was even a gay cowboy or two in my family, though this was not mentioned. Why hadn't I written that story myself? (There are a few who think I have, in the characters of Gus and Call.)

In any case, after I gave back the magazine, Diana suggested that it would make a wonderful movie and I agreed. Within the day we had a letter off to Annie Proulx, whom neither of us knew, offering a modest option payment for a chance to take a shot at "Brokeback" as a film.

We knew we had to hurry. That kind of material doesn't just sit around.

Shortly after Annie granted us the option a line began to form. It was several years before it was certain that Ang Lee would direct, that Heath Ledger, now tragically gone, would take the role of Ennis Del Mar, and so on. Nearly nine years passed before the two of us showed up at the Kodak Theatre, on Hollywood Boulevard, for the Oscar competition in 2006.

I'm sure that someday Diana herself will tell her own story about life in the movies, and the making of *Brokeback Mountain,* and my rather distant observation should not preempt her. She co-wrote and co-produced; she braved the mosquitoes of Alberta in midsummer; she fought through the many layers of movie studio administration; and, most importantly, she *saw* it all, whereas I, the man who disliked movie sets, only had a few meetings here in the Lower 48. In fact I wrote a book about Buffalo Bill, and another novel involving that extraordinary man, while cast and crew of *Brokeback* were struggling with the elements, and themselves, far to the north.

Diana should tell her version when she's ready. My purpose here is to write about Hollywood: the town and the culture rather than any given film. So, over to Diana, and lots of luck.

46

ANNIE PROULX, WHO lived at the time in the Medicine Bow, made two visits to my bookshop. On the second she bought something unusual: the bound newsletters of a firm in Fort Worth that specialized for decades in asphalt and industrial grease.

You don't sell many newsletters devoted to the problems of industrial grease.

Short chapter, sorry.

47

I HAVE NEVER been much interested in awards, despite having won more than my share. *Lonesome Dove* alone picked up about a dozen, and, since it's now in its twenty-fifth anniversary year, it may pick up one or two more.

Only one of these awards actually injured me, and that was when I won the Spur Award from the Western Writers of America. It was a real spur too, a big, sharp-tonged Mexican spur, which, as I was holding it up for inspection, slipped off its plaque and stuck briefly in my leg. Awards can be injurious to the recipient.

Later, in the remote town of Marfa, I won a chunk of pink lava, with a little lava Donald Judd cube on its roof. It's quite heavy, but I have a door that is now stopped by this handsome, if curious, piece of work.

I think of awards as a form of grading and I have never thought grading has much to do with art. Susan Sontag once claimed that grading actually held her back; she made such good grades that she went into adulthood believing that she was better than, in her estimation, she actually was.

Despite my personal attitude toward awards, I became a (reluctant) partner in about one dozen awards shows, accompanied always by Diana

Ossana, who has had a different life from me and richly deserved the many awards she got as writer-producer of *Brokeback Mountain*. She deserved them for another reason: without her efforts I don't believe that movie would have made it onto the screen.

The reason Diana won so many awards in only maybe a dozen awards ceremonies is because she won for both writing and producing. It seemed wrong to rain on my tenacious partner's parade, so I went and sat as in a trance through many long congratulatory evenings.

My own finest awards moment—better than getting the Oscar—was opening my eyes in the back of a limo one night just as we were passing the Troubadour, the famous rock club on Santa Monica Boulevard, and there, behold, was my son's name: James McMurtry, who either just played there or was about to.

That was an excellent thing for a father to see, out of one eye, in a limo in Los Angeles, in the middle of the night.

From the first I tended to treat these galas rather cavalierly, wandering off just when I was needed and dozing through most of the speeches. Finding the gents', always a problem in large gatherings, was even more of a problem at the Oscars and several other venues. It took all of our brilliant publicist's, Amanda Lundberg's, ingenuity, and the Focus Features team's as well, to get me where I was supposed to be when I was supposed to be there, but they did their gallant best. When Focus accepted the fact that we intended to keep our own girl in this horse race, things went smoothly enough, at least they did once we had mastered the strange anthropological rite of the Red Carpet, about which more later.

The first of these awards was held in the cavernous and tomblike Civic Auditorium in Santa Monica. We stepped on our first Red Carpet and went sailing into the world of eternal hype. The questions asked as we inched along the carpet were of no interest and our answers cannot have been much better.

This being a movie about gay ranch hands, we expected protesters, but in fact there was only one, who carried a little sign saying "No Homos on the Range." He looked sort of lonely. Ang and I wanted to go out and reason with him but were not permitted.

48

THIS, THE BROADCAST Film Critics Awards, was our very first awards ceremony and we we didn't really know what to do or say. For entertainment we listened to a little light chitchat between George Clooney and Julia Roberts, the former looking more and more like the Cary Grant *de nos jours*. Diana accepted the award for Michelle Williams, who was far away. We didn't expect to win and we didn't win the writing award but we *did* win best picture, which took us by surprise.

My own main worry was about finding our car in the melee after the show, but soon learned that well-trained kids—called wranglers—kept track of the limos and got us to ours safely. I could not but reflect that these limo wranglers were much more helpful than the real wranglers up in Alberta, who either did not know about sheeps' refusal to drink from flowing streams, or else just did not bother to pass what they knew on to their bosses, thus slowing production for part of a day.

In my judgment, the L.A. Film Critics Awards, held toward the end of the long parade of ceremonies, is by a large measure the most boring of the dozen shows. That particular ceremony was not televised—thus removing the last constraint on the egos of the film critics. So critic after critic rattled on about the virtues of some long-dead editor or sidekicks of various kinds.

We were five hours and fifteen minutes at table on this torturous occasion. Even the Oscars rarely take much longer than that. I went to the whole range of awards dinners without consuming a bite of food, mainly because what was on my plate in front of me didn't look edible. James Schamus, the head of Focus Features, was not so finicky—on more than one occasion he ate his food and—after asking—mine too.

Of course these soirees were kept under fair control if they were being televised. Air space, of course, is not free.

49

Except for the Oscars the most important of these awards was the Golden Globes, where the members of the Foreign Press get to vote for their favorites. The Foreign Press numbers in the hundreds—several hundreds—but still a lot less than the thousands who vote on the Oscars themselves.

If these ceremonies had a saving grace it was that we always won best picture—always, that is, up and until the final vote, where we lost to *Crash*. But our long row of successes must have been very deflating to everyone who lost. To sit through so much tedium and so much bombast and then *lose* must be nearly intolerable. We were always given mike-accessible tables, with the Clooney table on one side of us and DreamWorks on the other. Both tables bore their lot stoically, but they did not shoot out waves of happiness. Rupert Murdoch was there—okay, he owns Fox, but still. Why go to anything so awful? Maybe his young wife actually enjoys this sort of thing; maybe the newness hasn't worn off yet. Harvey Weinstein was there, and all the familar faces that in my judgment are easier to tolerate in the pages of *Variety* than when being crammed into an actual place. Jeffrey Katzenberg was more stoical than most. I reminded him of our Eddie Murphy picture and he had the grace to smile.

50

OF THE IMPORTANT awards the one we dominated was the Golden Globes. We won best picture, best director, best adapted screenplay, etc. . . . on and on. I gamely thanked my Hermes 3000 for my award, mentioning that for thirty years it had saved me from the dry embrace of the computer.

Harrison Ford, who presented our award, liked that and said, "Nicely put," as we walked offstage. Perhaps this small compliment caused me to forget my instructions, which were to follow Diana offstage and past a line of photographers and onto a line of journalists. Instead of enacting this simple ritual I veered off to the gents'—I never go by one without reflecting that I am sure to need it soon—and then went back to my table, thus screwing up the orderly practices of awards ceremony publicity. The little man who was supposed to line me up couldn't find me but seemed to think I might be in Harrison Ford's pocket, resulting in a very funny photo of the little man searching, and Harrison Ford trying to escape him, while Diana stands serenely by. The *L.A. Times*, below the fold, showed Diana, Harrison Ford, and the small man trying and failing to find me.

I was eventually located, photographed, and questioned. And Sara Ossana eventually found me as well.

In Los Angeles a mistake of that nature, if it happens to get your partner's picture on the front page of the *Times*, cannot be an entirely bad thing.

Another by-product of it is that it turned Tom Hanks into a collector of manual typewriters. I hear that he has more than one hundred now.

51

MY OWN MOST embarrassing moment occurred at the Writers Guild dinner, when I managed to flip my dessert plate in such a way as to cover my dress shirt with raspberry sorbet. This occurred to my horror while Diana was in the Ladies' and our presenter had just walked onto the stage. Fortunately Diana came racing into place, and if anyone noticed that I had apparently committed hara-kiri it certainly wasn't Dan Rather and George Clooney, who were seated just below me. Rather was there to give the Edward R. Murrow award to Clooney, who had just made his under-appreciated homage to Murrow—*Good Night, and Good Luck.*

Dan Rather was no longer an anchorman, and it was clear that he missed his old calling, talking rapidly to anyone he could corner.

I worried at most a half a minute over the matter of the sorbet. Egos so much greater than my own were loose in the room. On the way back to the hotel I pondered again what it must feel like to attend event after event and *lose?*

It wasn't something I wanted to try.

52

WE DON'T NORMALLY associate the late, great French leader Charles de Gaulle with merriment, but he was once heard to say that "One must take one's fun where one finds it." I have lost track of the biography in which that remark appears, but I certainly can agree with the general, while possibly adding the caveat that movie premieres and awards ceremonies, whether glossy or drab, are events where one is very unlikely to have anything that could accurately be called fun.

Previous to the chariot race of *Brokeback* I had only attended two premieres: a very modest one for *Hud* held in Fort Worth in 1963, and a more elaborate one in Hollywood for *The Evening Star,* which Diana and I and some friends more or less crashed. We may have been sent tickets to this bespangled event, but that doesn't mean we were made to feel welcome when we arrived. I have been told that differences abounded during the making of this strange film, one result of which was that Polly Platt was sent into exile, after which a general feeling of malaise held the production in its grip. The director was Robert Harling, the star was Shirley MacLaine, who about that time was the victim of a classic put-down, delivered by the late Walter Matthau. The put-down occurred at Irving Lazar's eightieth birthday party, held in Le Dome, a French restaurant on Sunset where Irving liked to hold court.

Diana, Sara, myself, Angie Dickinson, Walter Isaacson (then the editor of *Time*), were ticking off all the places we had flown in from. Angie Dickinson said Aspen, and we said Tucson when Shirley MacLaine came over and sat next to Walter Matthau, who looked at her skeptically and said, "Where did you fly in from, Uranus?" Shirley MacLaine did not respond.

I don't know her, but, a year later, while presenting an award, I was sitting alone in an old theater when a scaly hand suddenly grasped mine. It was Shirley, who was receiving an award for *The Evening Star*. "What do I say," she asked, "if they ask me why I wanted to play Aurora?"

Fortunately I had an answer ready.

"Well, it might be," I suggested, "because she always parks a yard from the curb so as not to scrape her tires."

That was good enough for Shirley, who used it in her speech.

53

THE ONE SIGNIFICANT thing that happened at the *Evening Star* premiere
was that I shook hands with Peter Bogdanovich for the first time since the
making of *Texasville,* over various loud fallings-out we had.

But this time he came with his daughters, whom I like. Peter was wear-
ing his same Serbian martyr's look, which I remember from the Oscarcast
of 1972. Grudges are normal, but to hold them forever, especially in a
town like Hollywood, where hundreds of people are apt to be holding
grudges, becomes silly. It can even become an obsession. So I went over to
Peter and said hello. He was, by this time, married (I think) to L.B., sister
of the late Dorothy Stratten.

I had met L.B. only glancingly, at one of my last visits to the mansion
on Copa De Oro.

Much later I heard that L.B., once the shooting of *Texasville* was over,
sometimes journeyed from the Bel Air villa to Wichita Falls, because she
found the malls in the latter place friendlier. Going from Bel Air to Wichita Falls, Texas, for the purpose of shopping, would probably make L.B.
unique on the planet.

However, there are other reasons for her to make the trip. One would
be that the villa on Copa De Oro was sliding down into ruin. Every time I
went it grew shabbier and shabbier.

I never heard L.B. speak of these visits but then I never really heard her speak at all.

Another possible explanation for L.B.'s shopping trips to the malls of Wichita Falls is that she simply found the Texans friendlier than the strange, seminocturnal creatures of Bel Air.

54

Brokeback Mountain was immediately recognized, even by people who didn't like it, to be a likely Oscar contender in several categories: best picture, best director, best adapted screenplay, best male actor . . . etc.

In my view we had the misfortune to be the front-runner for a couple of weeks too long. The newness wore off, and Hollywood can be just as bored with winners as they can with losers. We experienced a slight diminishment of momentum, though momentum had carried us far, but in the end in the best picture category we were nipped at the wire by *Crash*.

55

Nonetheless, from the late fall of 2005 we on the *Brokeback* team had a very hot picture to promote and release. We accordingly traveled to several premieres and semi-premieres. Journalists hoevered over us like locusts over a wheat field. We did one whole day of junket-type press in New York, and another whole day of television press in Austin.

There is, thankfully, only so much one can say about a given motion picture, and Diana and I and our teammates not only said it all, we said it all several dozen times.

We went to Denver, to open their new opera house. We went to Santa Barbara, to be welcomed, I guess. In Denver, Ang Lee met Annie Proulx, who (in Western terms) lived right up the road.

Then we did the big ones: New York and L.A. Diana and I stayed at New York's Regency, the hotel whose famous breakfast room I had been kicked out of for appearing in a turtleneck instead of a tie. This upset my host, Alan Pakula, but it didn't get me in the breakfast room, which seems to have relaxed a bit.

There the junketeers arrived, wave after wave, each allowed about fifteen minutes.

The New York premiere was packed and a consequence of the crush is that I somehow got swept into the executive's car, and ended up in the meatpacking district, where we were allowed to eat at Mario Batali's not yet opened new restaurant, which had so much floor space that one could have landed a DC-10 in it.

In the car, on my way back to join the rest of the team at a less surreal dining establishment, I happened to look up as we were crossing 24th Street and glimpsed the penthouse where my friend Susan Sontag once lived. It was her last home, and I was in it once and once only.

I didn't last long at the other post-premiere meal up the street.

56

THERE ARE SEVERAL awards to be had in America that would seem to come unbidden, in the sense that the winners don't have to apply, fill out forms, or do anything except appear to be pleasantly surprised that the award falls in their laps. The Pritzker Prize in architecture is one such and the MacArthur Genius Award is another. Presumably a secretive board of one's peers makes the choices and arranges for the money to be paid. There's no unseemly dog-eat-dog scratching and clawing, as there is sure to be during the Oscarcade: and likewise for the Emmys, Grammys, Tonys, etc.

The Oscar remains by far the most coveted of these showbiz awards, and it is also much the hardest to win.

I worked in blissful ignorance of how hard the Oscar is to win for a full fifty years of my time in the entertainment world, that is the screenwriting trade, without having any idea how hard it actually is to win an Oscar. It's true that I was nominated for an Oscar in 1972, for *Picture Show*, but I didn't go to any trouble, didn't expect to win, and of course didn't win. The veteran—in this case, as I've mentioned, Ernest Tidyman—won over the rookie.

I should quickly add that I didn't much try to win. If anyone was doing any awards dinners on behalf of *Picture Show* it was Peter Bogdanovich, not me. And, unlike Peter, I thought the award was fair—better to reward a veteran than two upstarts like Peter and me.

Of course there's the matter of art that one can factor in, if one wants to try. The best art *should* win: *Raging Bull,* not *Ordinary People; Reds,* not *Chariots of Fire;* and, probably, *The Last Picture Show,* not *The French Connection;* but any thinking based on the conviction that one movie is art and another not is purely speculative.

Only time will answer that question.

57

AFTER WE HAD been to five or six awards dinners—Directors Guild, Producers Guild, Golden Globes, etc.—I realized that all this, miserable as much of it was, was only a complex prelude to the Big Event—the Oscars—which were held rather early and staged at the famous Kodak Theatre on Hollywood Boulevard.

This was, let me tell you, a big event, so big that it even involved diverting traffic off the 101 Freeway, the major artery that slashes through Hollywood from north to south.

For an exit on the 101 to be even momentarily closed threatened patterns across the whole nation—there could be a ripple effect at least as far as Boston.

As the Oscar winner and veteran nominee Diane Keaton once told me, it takes a whole day to go to the Oscars. From an even broader perspective it can seem to take most of the fall and a good bit of the winter to get this spectacle staged.

Certainly it takes a whole day. The ladies, already beautiful, have to be turned by the miracles of Hair and Makeup that can be achieved; the budgets for this wizardry probably exceed the GNP of several small nations.

All the candidates need to think up, and maybe scribble down, graceful acceptance speeches thanking everyone they know. Sometimes this preparation is neglected, leaving a tongue-tied candid winner to stand silently in front of an audience of billions, with absolutely nothing to say.

I myself, as Oscar day wore on and the ladies were being transformed into goddesses, found myself worrying most about the reliability of limo drivers. Ours didn't appear quite on time and I became ever more nervous. I was reminded of the time when I had unaccountably been invited to the great White House dinner, hosted by the Reagans, for the Prince and Princess of Wales. My driver, a recent arrival from Kabul, not only couldn't find the White House, he had never heard of it, though he picked me up only sixteen blocks from it.

Our driver for the Oscars *did* show and delivered us so promptly that we were several hours early.

Dressing for the Oscars produced another problem. I had the jacket of a fine old tux, made for me by a wonderful tailor in D.C., a Hungarian Jew who made dress clothes for gentlemen in D.C. for many years.

I had the top, but had lost track of the bottom. But I had a very fresh pair of jeans, meaning I had the makings of what is called a Texas tux— dress shirt, bow tie, dinner jacket, and jeans and boots.

A Texas tux has the added virtue of being comfortable, no mean quality if one is going to be trapped in a narrow seat for five hours.

So I set sail into the Oscars with confidence ... and this confidence was not really misplaced, because my fresh, clean jeans, good dinner jacket, and polished boots were the hit of the evening—they even prompted the host, Jon Stewart, to make a snippy remark about my jeans.

58

On the Red Carpet, a curious anthropological rite about whose evolution I may someday write a short book, my jeans attracted as much attention as many a $5,000 gown.

The Oscar viewership has been iffy for several years, mainly because the event is simply too long. For some time now the technical Oscars have given their own awards dinner, as is only right. But some of the craft guilds, many of whose work is plenty technical, nonetheless want to be part of the Big Event, and too many of them have been kept in. The big Oscars are the real deal: perhaps the hardest competition in America's arts. I can certainly understand the technicians wanting to be part of the big show; but, in my opinion, too much of the technicians still *is* in and does much to slow down an already sluggish evening. Sound mixing is important but I still don't much enjoy listening to the sound mixers thanking everybody they know.

Though the producers of the Oscars did their best to create a vivid mixture of montage, music, and wit, they still, in my opinion, failed. Tom Hanks's skit didn't go off well, and Reese Witherspoon got lost for a while amid the sets. Fortunately she went on to win for *Walk the Line*; yet still the evening slogged. The audience was restive; what many elders such as myself had much on their minds was bladder control. Four and a half hours inched by, producing no big thrills for anyone, except perhaps the producers of *Crash*.

I was interested in the seat fillers, the adroit kids who slipped instantly into the seat left by those who had dared to dart to the bathroom. And then popped out again, to hover mysteriously until they were needed again. Their job was to make sure the cameras showed a full house.

Of course interest quickened as the big awards began to arrive: best actor and actress, best director, best picture, and so on. Many in our row were still working on their acceptance speeches, just in case such were needed.

Crash's eventual victory proved that it's easier to vote against drug dealers than for gay cowboys. It was, anyway, essentially a hometown movie, and one's hometown is easy to vote for: a good number of the talent in *Crash* was local, which didn't hurt.

I thought once the Oscars were over I could simply go home and relax into my old life, but it didn't prove to be that easy. Months of tension and anxiety were not immediately erased. The hardest to win creative award in America stays hard even after you've won it.

59

I'M SOMETIMES ASKED if I have much nostalgia for the Hollywood that existed fifty years ago. Was it more civil, less civil, about the same: my answer after thinking about it awhile is: about the same. Years ago, at the beginning of my screenwriting career, I normally wore a coat and tie to meetings. Now I normally wouldn't bother.

Some of the more elegant restaurants once had a dress code. I can't think of one that has one these days, although there could be a French place or two, hiding out now. Many, of course, prefer that their customers look nice.

The ascendancy of Michael Ovitz, when CAA was firing on all cylinders, did affect the marketing system for a while; agents who dealt with the biggest stars came to feel as though they might be stars themselves. The soldier characters—again I'll mention Ron Meyer—never lose sight of their roots in flesh peddling. The other highfliers were brought pretty much in line by the nature of the culture itself. They weren't, after all, stars: they just worked for actors who were stars.

When Michael Ovitz was on top he was a kind of pharaoh, and he summoned another pharaoh, I. M. Pei, to design his sepulchre, the cold white building that, no longer occupied by CAA or Ovitz, stands at the corner of Wilshire and Little Santa Monica, in Beverly Hills.

It's been my long-held view that that piece of real estate, that white building, is the coldest, least friendly place in Hollywood. It's a space designed by one cool pharaoh for another; the lobby is essentially a slave pen, where supplicants and slaves mill around aimlessly, while losing their grip on whatever hopes they may have come in with.

Only the biggest stars escape the purgatory of that lobby.

Diana and I were handled by CAA: our mistake, since if anything was obvious it was that CAA was not a writers' agency. As clients, though, we were trotted around to various production companies, none of which had the slightest interest in us.

We were not, after all, Michael Crichton, so why were we ever there?

After Ovitz's departure, Richard Lovett was head of the agency. We had, with CAA's sanction, mentioned my novel *Comanche Moon* to the director Michael Mann, who exhibited no interest at that time. A little later, though, I was to discover that a deal was in the works, involving Joe Roth, then at Disney, Michael Mann, and the excellent screenwriter Eric Roth.

Besides being a fine screenwriter, Eric Roth is a lot more expensive than we were at the time—I wish him the best—but there was one little wobble in this dream deal, and that was that I in fact owned the rights to the property.

Rarely shocked by Hollywood dealings, this time I was shocked. An agency arrogant enough to make two deals before they bother to acquire the rights to the property in question is an agency that doesn't realize that there is such a thing as going too far.

Time, I felt, to wake them up. I kept the rights to *Comanche Moon* and Diana and I kept most of the screenwriting money when it was eventually made for CBS.

Diana was an executive producer and oversaw the making of the miniseries, which was filmed in New Mexico.

The behavior of CAA in this one instance is as good an example as one needs of a failure in strategic thinking.

If Robert Bookman, CAA's man for literature, had come to me quietly and told me there might be something brewing with Disney about *Comanche Moon,* I might have been receptive. It would have depended on the state of our finances, and what else we had on our plate. You would think the leading talent agency in the world would have known that. But they had been used to dealing with that lobbyful of slaves too long, and so had forgotten the first rule of agentry: get the rights!

60

AFTER WE HAD collected our Oscars and passed through several thick fields of journalists on Oscar night, Diana and Sara and I parted ways. They were off to the parties, and I was headed for Santa Monica and bed. Our publicist, the gracious Amanda Lundberg, walked me over to my limo and, as it were, tucked me in.

Only after Amanda had vanished into the mob did it dawn on me that this wasn't *my* limo—it was for Diana and Sara, and was filled with stuff they might need in their partying.

Amanda had rushed back to her innumerable duties and I had not yet come to own a cell phone. The likelihood of there actually being a second limo waiting just for me seemed remote. The nice girls who kept up with limo flow consulted many lists, on none of which did they find my name.

I was dismayed for a minute or two, and then I ceased to be dismayed. After all, I was not lost—it was only a short stroll to my old haunts on Hollywood Boulevard, or Las Palmas or Wilcox, all places where there had once been bookshops galore and, furthermore, bookshops that had once been open almost all night, a literary feast for a Texas boy who once had been hard put to imagine that such wonders even existed.

I knew that, technically, Hollywood Boulevard was thought to be a risk at this hour, and probably was a risk. But I had known it a long time before and it was always a risk. Now it was a risk without bookshops, but, oh, the memories it held for me. Here had been the Heritage, when they moved in from Compton. Here had been the Pickwick, the great shop where Susan Sontag occasionally nipped Modern Library books, busing in from the Valley to find them.

I looked across the boulevard at the darkened form of Larry Edmunds Bookshop, whose general stock I had purchased in 1964. And, just off the boulevard was the storefront on Las Palmas where an irascible book scout known as Red had set up a little shop for a while.

Whatever it is now, Hollywood Boulevard is a fine street for a book scout to reminisce on.

I wandered down to the once fabulous intersection, Hollywood and Vine, where a nice cabbie took me in and drove me to the Casa del Mar, where I had a decent cheeseburger and slept to the sound of the sea.